Decolonial ARCHIVAL FUTURES

A joint publication of the Society of American Archivists and the American Library Association.

ALA Neal-Schuman purchases fund advocacy, awareness, and accreditation programs for library professionals worldwide.

Decolonial
ARCHIVAL
FUTURES

KRISTA McCRACKEN AND SKYLEE-STORM HOGAN-STACEY

FOREWORD BY RICARDO L. PUNZALAN

CHICAGO 2023

Series Editors

AMY COOPER CARY is Head of Special Collections and University Archives at Marquette University. She has served on editorial boards for *American Archivist*; *Archival Issues*; *RBM: A Journal of Rare Books, Manuscripts, and Cultural Heritage*; and *The Journal of Archival Organization*. She is a Fellow of the Society of American Archivists.

BETHANY ANDERSON is the Natural and Applied Sciences Archivist at the University of Illinois, Urbana-Champaign. She serves as Editor-in-Chief for *Comma, International Journal on Archives* and previously served as Reviews Editor for *American Archivist*. Anderson has a master's degree in Information Studies with a specialization in Archival Studies and Records Management from the University of Texas at Austin and a master's in Near Eastern Art and Archaeology from the University of Chicago.

© 2023 by Krista McCracken and Skylee-Storm Hogan-Stacey

Extensive effort has gone into ensuring the reliability of the information in this book; however, the publisher makes no warranty, express or implied, with respect to the material contained herein.

ISBN: 978-0-8389-3715-0 (paper)

Library of Congress Control Number: 2023937493

Book design by Kim Hudgins in the Chaparral Pro and Brandon Grotesque typefaces; cover image © Viktoriia/Adobe Stock.

♾ This paper meets the requirements of ANSI/NISO Z39.48-1992 (Permanence of Paper).

Printed in the United States of America
27 26 25 24 23   5 4 3 2 1

Contents

Series Introduction ... vii
Foreword ... ix
Preface ... xiii
Acknowledgments ... xix

1 Recognizing Colonial Frameworks   1
Colonial Archives in the United States ... 3
Colonial Archives in Canada ... 4
Colonial Archives in Australia ... 6
Colonial Archives in New Zealand ... 7
Moving Away from Colonial Archives ... 9

2 Archives and Cultural Protocols   13
UNDRIP and Archival Practice ... 14
Protocols in the United States ... 15
Protocols in Canada ... 18
Protocols in Australia ... 21
Protocols in New Zealand ... 23
Protocols in Practice ... 25

3 Challenging Original Order and Provenance   31
Indigenous Provenance in the United States ... 33
Indigenous Provenance in Canada ... 35
Indigenous Provenance in Australia ... 37
Indigenous Provenance in New Zealand ... 38
Digital Approaches to Provenance ... 40

4 **Community-Based Archival Description**   45

    American Participatory Description and Community Archives...48

    Canadian Participatory Description and Community Archives...49

    Australian Participatory Description and Community Archives...51

    New Zealand Participatory Description and Community Archives...54

    Approaching Decolonizing Description...56

5 **Indigenous Archival Futures**   61

    Areas for Transformation of Archival Practice...64

Bibliography...69
About the Authors...81
Index...83

Series Introduction

"WHAT'S PAST IS PROLOGUE": IN *THE TEMPEST*, SHAKESPEARE REMINDS us that our actions up to this very moment provide context for our present decisions and actions. The accrual of this activity, in the form of the archival record, enables us to reflect on that past with tangible evidence in hand (or on screen). But recorded evidence doesn't just enable us to interrogate the present. We preserve the records and data of the present to provide evidence and context that will help us shape our collective future.

The Archival Futures series seeks to capture an irony that lies at the heart of the series title: Can what is past have a future, and vice versa? As a point of departure for critical thinking and for conversation, it centers the active role of archivists *and* everyday people in documenting society. Above all, it seeks to bring together all individuals who have a vested interest in cultural heritage and its stewardship, to both acknowledge and imagine the importance of the future archival record. This is a tall order.

When people find themselves without records and archives, memory, accountability, and transparency become precarious. We all share a collective, vested interest in the future of archives and must be partners in the preservation of the evidence of our present. Archivists act on behalf of the public good. Our work is focused outward and reflects the interests of many individuals and institutions. When archivists appraise records for enduring archival value, we imagine how people will use those materials; when archivists arrange and describe those records, we imagine how those descriptions might help people access important records; when archivists select technology and systems to serve as interfaces to our inventories and digital materials, we consider the ease with which people can find critical information; when archivists preserve and provide access to records, we imagine how those records will provide context for complex issues to society in the future; and when archivists consider the constellation of digital content on the Web—social media, hosted systems, local systems—and the fragility and ephemeral nature of that content, we understand our vital roles as stewards for the historical record and our role in ensuring that these materials will exist in the future.

What makes this engagement of the archival record possible is a new approach to looking at the archival endeavor. By considering the work of archivists along with the theory that underpins that work, and by pairing that with ideas from contemporary trends in social theory, this series shows how the preservation and stewardship of the archival record is a collective effort that underpins and supports inclusive and democratic societies and institutions. Our current times stand as a watershed for transparency, authenticity, accountability, and representation. These values are bound to the responsible preservation of our historical materials, and everyone should be concerned with the processes by which we accomplish this.

The decision to preserve a historical record is also undertaken in conjunction with allied professionals, such as librarians, museum curators, and information scientists, and is fundamentally future oriented. As the contributions to this series reveal, the notion of an *archival future* underlies all discussions concerning the responsibility to promote the preservation of records that document the full range of human activity. Archival practice necessarily responds to the past, the present, and the future. Archival professionals imagine a future—whether in the next century or a week from now—and strive to support the use of records in that future, by people not yet known, for reasons not yet imagined.

Through the contributions to this series, we want to open the discussion about the future of the archival record. We enter into this with the understanding that the archival record of the past informs contemporary society and that archival practice is a collaborative endeavor—between archivists, librarians, and people. Our stake in the future is written in the records and archives that represent us and tell our stories to future generations. What is past is not simply prologue; what is present is not simply epilogue; the records of the now are vital to the future of human society.

Amy Cooper Cary
Bethany Anderson

Foreword

"[WE] HAVE WORK TO DO"—WORK TO DECOLONIZE ARCHIVES AND build better community relationships. With their deep engagement in grassroots, Indigenous community archives, Krista McCracken and Skylee-Storm Hogan-Stacey know a thing or two about decolonial work and the liberative promise that this work holds for the future of archives—our collective future. And we—"archivists, the archives profession, and archival organizations"— must listen.[1] They are right when they say that "[we] have work to do," and they show us the tools and ideas that we can use to accomplish the work of decolonization.

Decolonial Archival Futures outlines the contexts of, and paths toward, decolonization. We must respond with enthusiasm and action. The book traces colonial legacies of archives in the United States, Canada, Australia, and New Zealand—countries that share related histories of settler colonialism. A notable contribution of this book is its comparative examination of the progress and challenges of these countries in the development and adoption of their respective protocols for stewarding Indigenous archival collections and building reciprocal relationships between institutions and source communities. McCracken and Hogan-Stacey pay close attention to implications of the United Nations Declaration on the Rights of Indigenous Peoples (UNDRIP) in reshaping archival work, eschewing Western knowledge systems, and embracing Indigenous knowledge and values. They have established this comparative backdrop to argue for the necessity of expanding archival notions of provenance, original order, and, by extension, custody and ownership. More profoundly, their emphasis on the involvement of Indigenous communities in all aspects of archival work, including participatory and reparative description, is a key step in Indigenizing archives and realizing a decolonial future.

I have a complicated and ambivalent relationship with archival ideas, having received my formative archival education in a former Spanish and American colony from a curriculum imported from US and European traditions. I began my career questioning the colonial foundations of archival thinking and the practices that those records encourage, but, at the same time, I believed in the power of archives and archivists to transform people's lives, histories, and imaginations. Over the years, I have seen the skepticism in embracing the message of community archives, the dismissive attitudes around reparative description, the outright belittling of community-based scholarship, and the objections to the Protocols for Native American Archival Materials (PNAAM). A common thread in all of these is that they all challenge professional canons of authority, control, and archival norms. As this book argues, we must learn how to confront our own discomfort in challenging colonial archival ideas. This is part and parcel of contemporary archival work that we all, not just a select some, must do to achieve a decolonial future.

Indeed, "[we] have work to do" when it comes to facilitating community engagement and establishing reciprocal relationships. I write this foreword after recently cofacilitating a visit of Filipino Indigenous artists to three repositories at the University of Michigan (U–M)—the Bentley Historical Library, the Special Collections Research Center, and the Museum of Anthropological Archaeology—as well as to the Newberry Library and the Field Museum in Chicago. The presence of Indigenous archives and material culture from the Philippines, as a former American colony, in the United States demonstrates and further complicates the issues discussed in this book considering the US histories of slavery, settler colonialism, and imperial expansions. For more than a century, archives and material culture that can be essential in sustaining cultural practices, languages, and relations have been far removed from the communities of the United States' former colony in the Pacific that need them most.

Bringing Indigenous culture bearers from the Cordillera region of the Northern Philippines—a basket weaver, a tattoo artist, and a textile master weaver—to examine and retrace the traditional artistic expressions of their ancestors showed U–M archivists and academics the power of direct community access and engagement. But even more, they showed the limitations of archival representation. As experts on their own history and culture, these visiting artists corrected many instances of misspellings, misattributions, and mislabels, thus underscoring McCracken and Hogan-Stacey's point about the crucial role of community experts in reshaping archival work, particularly in the area of archival description. U–M's archives, libraries, and museums could update our finding aids, but in some cases, we were not prepared to navigate the visitors' emotions of such encounters despite numerous articles on archival trauma and re-traumatization in the reading room. Community collaboration and willingness to change harmful practices are particularly potent for the future work with Philippine archives that U–M hopes to do, namely building reciprocal stewardship relationships between Indigenous Filipinos, archivists, and archival repositories.

When there is harm, there is pain. McCracken and Hogan-Stacey are right when they say, "[we] have work to do" that will require "active engagement, difficult conversations, meaningful partnerships, and change."[2] Encountering traditional aesthetics, patterns, and designs in photographs and manuscripts produced in the context of colonial administration and scholarship, which have been carefully preserved in US archives but inaccessible to communities they document, brought up complex emotions with our Filipino visiting artists. On one hand, these materials were gathered or produced at the height of colonial rule, and they indeed reflect the period when they were used to justify colonialism and racist policies, but they are also sources for examining cultural/historical knowledge of many communities in the present.

In my pursuit of community-based research that facilitates access and use of archives, I have seen firsthand the discomfort and pain of relying on colonial records to retrace or sustain traditional knowledge. Indigenous cultural expressions and lifeways have been a frequent target of (unsuccessful) colonial annihilation. We have so much work to do to support, honor, and celebrate the survivance[3] of Indigenous communities, despite continuing legacies of unspeakable colonial violence. McCracken and Hogan-Stacey begin to explore the many layers of work that will be required. An unknown, and often unacknowledged, record of Indigenous Peoples' cultural memory is kept in archival repositories, stewarded in some cases by archivists who lack sufficient cultural knowledge about them or the resources to ethically represent that knowledge. There are times when we must acknowledge that despite (and often, because of) our best intentions and allegiance to professional standards, we fail and (un)wittingly replicate harm to communities. After reading this book, it will be more difficult for anyone to take a neutral stance or adhere to principles and practices that our scholarship has proven to be, at best, out of touch with our changing cultural, social, and technical landscapes.

I believe in the message of *Decolonial Archival Futures*. Archives are as much about the past as about their significance in the present. We must act now so we have some hope of creating the decolonial archival futures that we want. Where there is harm, we must work diligently toward repair. When community perspectives are ignored, we must adopt more inclusive description and policies. When community access is systemically denied, archivists must question these policies and, when possible and appropriate, cede control. And because archival thinking and policy are colonial, we must work toward transformation and Indigenization. This book underscores the first steps to repair the many decades of lack of community control over archives and to build the relationships that are a necessary foundation for a reciprocal model of stewardship. We have work to do.

Ricardo L. Punzalan
University of Michigan School of Information

NOTES

1. Krista McCracken and Skylee-Storm Hogan-Stacey, *Decolonial Archival Futures* (Chicago: ALA Neal-Schuman and Society of American Archivists, 2023), 61.
2. McCracken and Hogan-Stacey, *Decolonial Archival Futures*, 61.
3. See Gerald Robert Vizenor's *Manifest Manners: Postindian Warriors of Survivance* (Hanover, CT: Wesleyan University Press, 1994); *Survivance: Narratives of Native Presence* (Lincoln, NE: University of Nebraska Press, 2008), and *Native Provenance: The Betrayal of Cultural Creativity* (Lincoln, NE: University of Nebraska Press, 2019).

Preface

MUCH OF THIS BOOK DRAWS ON OUR DIRECT EXPERIENCE WORKING in Indigenous community archives and with Indigenous communities. We believe it is essential to clearly articulate our positionality in relation to the Indigenous communities we are writing about.

I (Krista McCracken) am a settler who lives on Robinson-Huron Treaty territory in Sault Ste. Marie, Ontario, Canada. Since 2010, I have worked at the Shingwauk Residential Schools Centre (SRSC), a grassroots community archives dedicated to preserving residential schools' legacy. I am extremely grateful for the opportunities I've had to work alongside residential school Survivors and Indigenous communities, and I continue to learn by listening to Elders and Survivors. When I started working at the SRSC in 2010, I thought I knew about archiving and how archives were supposed to work. But I wasn't prepared to work in a community archives. Canadian archival standards hadn't prepared me for working with community, prioritizing community needs over archival standards. Survivors and Elders showed me a lot of kindness in my early days at the SRSC, where they gently but firmly told me that what I had learned in school was wrong. Their words continue to guide me as I learn to be a more supportive archivist and work to serve community the best I can.

I (Skylee-Storm Hogan-Stacey) am an urban Indigenous person, descended from the Mohawk Nation of Kahnawà:ke paternally and from settlers maternally. I have spent most of my life between the Greater Tkaronto (Toronto) Area, Tiohti:áke (Montreal), and Baawaating (Sault Ste. Marie). Throughout my career, I have held various positions with the SRSC, and this experience continues to shape my current scholarship, research, and work, which involves advising and writing public history projects. I completed my master of arts degree in history, specializing in public history, with the University of Western Ontario's Public History program in 2019. My focus with that program was building the skills necessary to understand and reconceptualize public history practice through a decolonial lens. After my degree, I found work as a historian with a historical services and research firm based in Ottawa, Ontario, Canada. My projects use archival collections for Indigenous historical and cultural research. As an Indigenous historian and researcher, I often reflect on privilege, access, and control of information. I also reflect on how archives work can leave archivists and historical researchers with vicarious trauma from the ways records are organized and described, as well as their contents. I have branched out from these experiences into policy analysis on behalf of federal government projects dedicated to reshaping archival systems and access for records associated with residential schools in Canada.

We share this information to situate ourselves, our perspectives, and our relationship to archival practice. How we work with communities and our own experiences working in archives and public history inform much of this book. The impetus for the book came from ongoing collaboration and conversations between us. Since our initial time working together in the SRSC, we have spent countless hours discussing the nature of archives and the relationship of Indigenous communities to archival practice. This book represents a continuation of this conversation to provide insight into the colonial roots of archives. It also examines Indigenous community archives and concepts of Indigenous community knowledge that actively resist colonial recordkeeping practices internationally. This book highlights the benefits and challenges of shifting archival narratives away from colonial recordkeeping practices, and it recenters community voices with practical examples. We aim to rethink the archival approach from a decolonized lens and challenge settler readers to critically examine archival power, including relationships with Indigenous knowledge keepers, Indigenous communities, and records documenting Indigenous peoples' lives.[1] When we identify members of the settler community, we want to clarify that this does not include descendants of enslaved persons brought to colonial states against their wishes or under false pretenses. Further, this does not include those who have immigrated to colonial states as refugees or out of necessity to preserve their lives or the lives of their families. We do not include those who have not benefited from the settler-colonial system of white supremacy and are a part of a growing diaspora marginalized by the settler-colonial state.

Settler colonialism is a particular type of colonialism that emphasizes a "logic of elimination and a structure of invasion."[2] Settler colonialism enacts itself through recordkeeping practices that erase and minimize Indigenous peoples' voices, experiences, and agency. By examining archival practices that actively counter settler colonialism, this book challenges non-Indigenous practitioners to consider constructs of knowledge, which histories we tell, and how we present the past. Further, the authors acknowledge that *decolonization* and *reconciliation* are both terms that have garnered substantial discussion within historical and archival scholarship. The work of Eve Tuck and K. Wayne Yang points to the complexity of decolonization and the need to articulate clearly what we mean when we use this term. The overuse of the term *decolonization* has impacted its meaning—the term is often attached to preexisting frameworks of social justice rather than its connection to Indigenous realities amid settler colonialism.[3] For the purposes of this book, decolonization is understood to mean accountability to Indigenous peoples. It is directly connected to Indigenous sovereignty and knowledges. Being accountable to Indigenous peoples means working with and alongside Indigenous communities to manage, understand, and work with archival records connected to, by, or about Indigenous peoples. Accountability to Indigenous peoples also involves a willingness to respect and act on Indigenous feedback, engage meaningfully in difficult conversations, and have a commitment to dismantling colonial power dynamics. Every community holds different perspectives based on their experiences, so it is key for decolonial archival practice to build relationships in a good way with the communities most impacted by the collections.

Decolonization should be viewed as approaching systems with Indigenous knowledge frameworks, considering and positioning Indigenous communities as leaders within those frameworks. This understanding of decolonization is important to us, the authors, as most colonial structures cannot be decolonized. With this in mind, decolonization offers a way to focus on the Indigenization of systems and moves beyond existing structures of colonialism. Decolonial archival practice within Indigenous knowledge frameworks directly ties itself to land, knowledge, sovereignty, and Indigenous leadership. The act of thinking about and consciously changing how historical knowledge is produced, communicated, and preserved is the work of decolonial archival and historical practice. This is discussed and expanded on throughout this book with particular emphasis on following Indigenous knowledge frameworks.

We have chosen to focus our writing on unsettling Western archival paradigms from the United States, Canada, New Zealand, and Australia. These four countries were selected because of their similar colonial pasts and the nature of recordkeeping in each country. The countries are all directly tied to the legacy of British colonialism and are all English speaking. Additionally, the selected countries were the only four to initially oppose the United Nations Declaration on the Rights of Indigenous Peoples (UNDRIP). The authors use UNDRIP throughout the book as a benchmark for archival engagement with Indigenous peoples but understand that not all Indigenous scholars see UNDRIP as a solution. These four countries have undertaken similar attempts at developing guidelines for archival care of Indigenous materials. However, these guidelines have been implemented on an ad hoc basis, and each country still has a significant amount of work to do to develop reciprocal archival relationships with Indigenous communities. Within the context of Canada and the United States, archival power is critical in the ongoing investigation of the mass graves attributed to the residential or boarding school system. The authors wish to acknowledge that phrasing the graves attributed to residential schools as a "recent discovery" discounts the oral histories and testimonies of Survivors and their families about the deaths of relatives and classmates from neglect and cruelty at these schools. In Canada, the government, in partnership with different religious denominations, administered residential schools as part of assimilationist policies.[4] In the United States, the church and government operated boarding schools through similar partnerships, but there is less information on which Christian denominations ran schools.[5] Archives have an essential role in supporting communities to locate missing children and the parties responsible.

As authors, we recognize that the United States, Canada, New Zealand, and Australia are not the only countries with a history of colonialism, nor are they the only countries where archival communities need to reexamine their relationship with Indigenous communities. Instead, this book offers a starting point for discussing decolonial archival practices on a global scale. We need flexible, clear guidelines on how to approach decolonial archival practice, and we need this practice to be taught in postsecondary settings and workplaces. We are not there yet. There remain tremendous gaps in educational settings in teaching about Indigenous archival practices and Indigenous ways of knowing.

Divided into five chapters, *Decolonial Archival Futures* moves from reflecting on colonial recordkeeping practices to imagining Indigenous archival futures. The opening chapter discusses the colonial roots of the United States, Canada, Australia, and New Zealand. It positions the legacy of colonialism in connection to recordkeeping and archival practice in each respective chapter. Chapter two is framed within the principles of self-determination and ownership and examines how UNDRIP relates to archival practice. This chapter also highlights the cultural stewardship protocols developed by each of the four countries, reflecting on the successes and challenges of these protocols. Chapters three and four are rooted in case study examples of Indigenous community archival practice. Chapter three looks at the principle of archival provenance and how original order and provenance can be reframed or reworked to meet the needs of Indigenous communities. Chapter four discusses participatory archival description and the integration of Indigenous communities in archival description practices. The book concludes with a forward-facing chapter in which the authors reimagine a future where archival practice, research, and community engagement exist within a decolonized, Indigenous-led framework.

Krista McCracken
Skylee-Storm Hogan-Stacey

NOTES

1. The term *settler* refers to non-Indigenous peoples who have, or whose ancestors have, settled in a land that Indigenous peoples have traditionally inhabited. Settlers have historically and continue to assert sovereignty over Indigenous land. For more information, see Emma Battell Lowman and Adam J. Barker, *Settler: Identity and Colonialism in 21st Century Canada* (Halifax: Fernwood Publishing Co. Ltd., 2015).
2. See Patrick Wolfe's "Settler Colonialism and the Elimination of the Native," *Journal of Genocide Research* 8 (2006): 387–409.
3. Eve Tuck and K. Wayne Yang, "Decolonization Is Not a Metaphor," *Decolonization: Indigeneity, Education & Society* 1, no. 1 (2012): 1–40.
4. Truth and Reconciliation Commission of Canada, *Canada's Residential Schools: The History, Part 1, Origins to 1939: The Final Report of the Truth and Reconciliation Commission of Canada*, Volume 1 (McGill-Queens University Press, 2015): 9–10.
5. Peter Smith, "US Report Details Church-State Collusion on Native Schools," Associated Press, May 14, 2022, https://apnews.com/article/canada-religion-education-native-americans-cultures-87a09745351c02236b99e2955785e1f7, captured at https://perma.cc/K8AM-38B3.

Acknowledgments

WE WISH TO THANK THE CHILDREN OF SHINGWAUK ALUMNI ASSOCIation for their ongoing support, resilience, and wisdom. The Children of Shingwauk Alumni Association have been actively decolonizing archival practice since the first Shingwauk Reunion in 1981. Their work has significantly shaped our perspectives on community archives and archival practice.

1

Recognizing Colonial Frameworks

SITUATED IN THE CONTEXT OF THE ARCHIVAL PRACTICE CONCERNING the colonial histories of the United States, Canada, Australia, and New Zealand, this chapter illustrates the ways in which archival structures have reinforced colonial relationships. These four countries are the focus of this book because of their connection to Indigenous communities, their shared British colonial pasts, and the current trends in community archives in each country. We recognize that some of the colonial policies and archival practices pre-date the formation of these four countries and are tied to colonial powers such as Britain. Each of these countries has robust state-run archives that documents settlement, government policy, settlers' lives, and the lives of Indigenous communities. In order to move toward a decolonial archival practice, the context of how these archives have formed, how they are still in use today, and how they shape historical and present narratives about Indigenous peoples needs to be understood. It is also important to look at how archival practice is taught, as it needs to be decolonized if the archival system is to be changed. Postsecondary programs focused on archives and libraries teach standardized organizational practices that serve the purposes of colonial institutions where their graduates hope to become employed. These programs sometimes have optional courses in Indigenous research methods, but this is rare and often not a required course. These programs also reproduce colonial systems of power through their faculty representation—with very few library science programs in Canada or the United States employing Indigenous faculty. Because the graduates of these programs are trained to replicate colonial systems, this continues once graduates enter the workforce. Documents used to shape the historical narratives of Indigenous peoples and the colonial state continue to be understood and archivally arranged from the colonial view.

The archives historically and contemporarily legitimize colonial states. The archives act as proof of what belongs and does not belong to the colonial state.[1] In the cases of government archives or archives of government-run institutions within countries with ongoing colonialism, these archives serve the needs of the colonizing power. Colonialism, particularly settler colonialism, is not a historical event. It is part of the ongoing treatment of Indigenous peoples. It is evident in the theft and redistribution of Indigenous land into settler property and the treatment of Indigenous peoples by governments.[2] We see colonialism in government legislation such as the Indian Act in Canada and in the reserve systems, set up across colonial countries to control Indigenous peoples, their rights, and their access to land while legitimizing colonial settlement within their imposed legal systems.[3] Settler-colonial government archives in the United States, Canada, Australia, and New Zealand document government initiatives, government programs, financials, population statistics, treaties with Indigenous nations, and broadly their relationships with Indigenous peoples. Colonial powers and their resulting archives keep track of all aspects, including the settlement and assimilation of their colonial countries. Part of this documentation includes extensive materials about the Indigenous populations. We find the lives, cultures, and histories of Indigenous peoples in these materials. Archives in settler-colonial states center the colonial population and legitimize the state as the forever occupier by establishing and preserving the legacy of the colonial power. Archives inform historical scholarship, and as pointed out by Michel-Rolph Trouillot, "[a]t best, history is a story about power, a story about those who won."[4] Archives are power laden in how they collect material, organize, and whose histories they represent. Archives are never neutral and always reflect selected narratives either through the records themselves, their description, or their organizational structure. Likewise, "[a]rchival power authorizes specific forms of the future by domiciling space and time, the here and now relative to the there and then; us as opposed to them."[5] Scholars and historians often use archives as evidence to support what happened when and where and create definitive narratives of the past. Archives control the past, and by doing so, they control imagined futures. Archives of settler-colonial states operate from a Western form of knowledge and recordkeeping. Because Indigenous and non-European forms of knowledge do not rely on the written word or depend on linear time, settler-colonial archives have ignored and marginalized these forms of knowledge and organization.[6]

The origins of modern-day archives and archival practice are commonly traced to the French Revolution. Indeed, J. J. Ghaddar and Michelle Caswell found that classical archival studies programs emphasize the connection between archives and "public governance, democratic accountability, national historiography, and the forging of a national or collective identity"[7] without directly recognizing that their management is inherently colonial, imperial, and rooted in white supremacy. State-run archives follow conventions established by dominant colonial groups within the power dynamics that exist within wider society. Access and an understanding of archival structures in colonial spaces require proximity to colonial knowledge systems and an understanding of the structures of colonialism and white supremacy.[8]

Colonial Archives in the United States

Colonial archives exist in state-run and private archives in the United States. The largest and most prominent example of an archives connected to colonial structures in the United States is the National Archives and Records Administration (NARA). NARA was formally established in 1934, but their collections date back to 1775, and they primarily hold materials of interest to the colonial state.[9] This includes materials as diverse as military records, ship manifests of the enslaved, naturalization records, founding documents, census rolls, and treaties with Indigenous peoples. Government departments across the United States maintain records of land treaties with Indigenous nations, and these records legitimize the land holdings of the United States and impact how Indigenous history is viewed today.[10] At this time, there is no information on how to search NARA's catalog for materials connected to specific tribes or communities or how to search for records tied to a geographic region. NARA is currently working to develop and improve these access points for researchers looking for materials related to specific time periods or Indigenous nations in the United States.[11] Researchers are currently told to "check back soon" for this access.[12] NARA does have a brief research guide on researching an American Indian individual or family.[13] This guide is fairly standard and directs people to learn more about census records, Bureau of Indian Affairs records, school records, employment records, and military records. The guide also acknowledges that "[l]ocating the records can prove tricky due to the continual changes in reservations, tribes, and geographic areas."[14] Colonial archives were not designed to support Indigenous community research, and often searching for information about an Indigenous person can be like searching for a needle in a haystack. There is a need for further expansion of resources to support Indigenous users of NARA, with additional research guides, more digitization, and directed assistance. A lack of access tools around what types of Indigenous records are available negatively impacts Indigenous communities and their ability to manage, document, and preserve their own history. The NARA website also notes that very few of the records related to Indigenous peoples in America have been digitized and made available, meaning that Indigenous community members are not able to access these records from their homes but would need to travel to see them.[15] Alternative ways of accessing archival records held by NARA are important for Indigenous peoples, many of whom are represented in the archival record but may not have the resources to physically access these materials.

The United States archives that house Indigenous boarding school records again replicate the power dynamics and hierarchies of American society.[16] In the case of boarding school records, researchers are often required to ask for specific records with no descriptions or lists provided for the schools. This means they need to already know specific things about staff or administration to make a request.[17] The purpose of archives connected to boarding schools in the United States was for use by administration and government authorities, not the students or their families. Proximity to colonial power is needed to navigate research associated with boarding schools. Knowledge to navigate these archives, and other archives, would only be available from those colonial viewpoints and therefore recreates colonial power dynamics. As Audre Lorde has noted, "The true focus of revolutionary change is never merely the oppressive situations which we seek to escape, but that piece of the oppressor which is planted deep within each of us, and which knows only the oppressors' tactics, the oppressor' relationships."[18] Changing archival systems involves changing the way we think as archivists, individuals, and people tied to colonial systems. Archival organizational system structures were designed to prioritize the colonial worldview, and therefore white supremacy. To center the white gaze is to understand the colonial archives. Despite how much documentation they contain regarding Indigenous peoples, states did not design archives to serve Indigenous communities—rather, they were designed to serve the state and document the state's paternal relationship with Indigenous peoples and the state's access to land for profit and settlement. The nature of creating the documents themselves, combined with how archives arrange and describe records, furthers the relationship between white supremacy and archives.

Colonial Archives in Canada

Much like NARA, Canada's national archives—Library and Archives Canada—serves as a repository for statistical and government information, but also serves as a cultural heritage resource to promote nation building and a sense of national identity.[19] These archives also connect to Indigenous dispossession and settler colonialism. Many collections and correspondence held within Library and Archives Canada confirm the government's mission of colonialism and assimilation outright. Library and Archives Canada contains records documenting treaties, the reserve system, the Department of Indian Affairs and its relationships to communities and peoples, daily life, Indigenous culture, reserve lands, and the administration of programs. These programs include the child welfare policies that implemented residential schools, day schools, and the Sixties Scoop.[20] These collections also document correspondence that assesses the progress of colonization, assimilation, and dispossession of lands as a measurement of progress. When describing the legacy of Canada's national archives, J. J. Ghaddar has noted,

> Built on stolen land, the Canadian national archives are full of records containing Indigenous information, knowledge, histories, and cultural expressions that have been revealed, acquired, or exposed because of colonization. One consequence of colonialism, then, is Indigenous people's lack of control over how their information, histories, and cultural knowledge are used and interpreted.[21]

Settler-colonial states, including Canada, have generated immense bodies of records about Indigenous peoples. However, those records have often been created without the consent of Indigenous communities, and they are structured without the use of communities in mind. Officials collected records to benefit governments administering programs or keeping track of how many people were owed under treaties. Additionally, collecting materials about Indigenous communities was often framed around preserving Indigenous history from vanishing, reinforcing the myth of the disappearing Indigenous communities, and not acknowledging the lived experiences of Indigenous peoples. Specifically, "archival photographs of Indigenous peoples have perpetuated misconceptions of a vanishing race or a long-forgotten people, even as their Indigenous cultures, customs, and heritage endured then as well as today."[22] Indigenous peoples have not vanished. They have had their lives fundamentally changed by colonial assimilationist agendas, but they are still here. Zoe Todd and Crystal Fraser have argued that although "Indigenous people are present in historical records, they are often depicted as passive bystanders, rarely free agents in their own right and far removed from narratives that highlight agency or sophistication."[23] The ways in which Indigenous peoples are presented in archives is colonial, often clouding the true realities of Indigenous life. Library and Archives Canada and its predecessor, the National Archives, were established to preserve the history of Canada; this was done at the expense of the histories of Indigenous peoples. Canadian archives are tied directly to colonialism and cannot escape this relationship.

Colonial Archives in Australia

Australia's archives and the National Archives of Australia (NAA) are rooted in a very similar colonial past as those of the United States and Canada. Versions of the NAA date back to 1913, with a standalone NAA being established and codified into law in 1983.[24] Indigenous peoples have often been the subject of archival records, without agency to control how those records are kept, shared, or used. When discussing the negative impact of state collecting and archiving practices in Australia, Natalie Harkin has remarked, "I travel through my own Nanna's records and recognise that we have never lived outside the State, and this very act of recognition continues the wounding. State acts of surveillance, recording and archiving had the power to place our family stories in the public domain, or obliterate stories within a broader history of erasure; filed away, silent and hidden until bidden."[25] Archives have taken culture, experiences, and history away from the control of Indigenous peoples in Australia. They have taken the lived experiences of Indigenous peoples and overdocumented them, put them in government-run archives, and made them accessible to the public. This includes records of displacement, children being removed from family,[26] and general overdocumentation of daily family life. This form of documentation is harmful to individuals, families, and communities. Indeed McKemmish, Faulkhead, and Russell have argued that:

> Australia's mainstream discourse and collective memory relating to Indigenous Australia have largely been built on the actions of a violent past, utilizing systems of remembering and forgetting that have supported a negative construction of Indigeneity within that collective memory. There is a pressing need for Australia's collective knowledge spaces to be reconfigured to be representative of all cultural voices.[27]

Australia's archives have been shaped by colonialism, and the country is beginning to reckon with this legacy and what it means for archives. There is still a lot of work to be done. For example, only one comprehensive archives guide relating to Indigenous peoples in the NAA exists, despite the large number of colonial records that document the lives of Indigenous peoples. The existing guide, for the archival records created by the Royal Commission into Aboriginal Deaths in Custody, is comprehensive, but it needs others like it.[28] Likewise, the Bringing Them Home name index, which contains the names of Aboriginal and Torres Strait Islander people, is not easily accessible to community members—community members need to contact archives staff to have them search the resource, which then points them to records that have to be requested.[29] This mediated access to records creates barriers for Aboriginal and Torres Strait Islander people, especially those who are unsure of the archival process or resistant to working with state institutions. The structural and "traditional" colonial protocols to access are counterintuitive to how Indigenous peoples share knowledge and access their histories. Placing colonial structures within the colonial archives has Indigenous peoples once again asking non-Indigenous peoples for access to things that should be theirs by inherent right.

Colonial Archives in New Zealand

Much like the United States, Canada, and Australia, New Zealand archives are intertwined with the colonial powers that gave them structure. Archives in New Zealand hold cultural and intellectual knowledge of Indigenous nations recorded by the state and record the transgressions the state would like to omit in courts of law today. Evelyn Wareham has noted that in the Pacific region, "[t]he cultural dimension of colonization is reflected in the alienation of knowledge and culture, along with land, forests, fisheries, and other physical property."[30] The push for increased open archival access grew with the research carried out during the first decade of the Waitangi Tribunal. The Waitangi Tribunal is a primary force for reconciliation in New Zealand. It was established as a permanent inquiry commission in 1975 to investigate violations of the Treaty of Waitangi.[31] The Tribunal reports and investigates issues related to treaty claims on an ongoing basis. Membership of the Tribunal is appointed by the Governor-General, based on recommendations from the Minister for Māori Development, and about half of the membership is Māori.[32] The Waitangi Tribunal was given special powers in 1985 to investigate breaches of the Treaty that dated back as far as 1840.[33] This work required the use and interpretation of archival materials. Of course, this was a challenge due to the nature of colonial archival structures.

New Zealand's archives and their history of replicating colonial power dynamics and structure do not differ much from other colonial states like the United States, Canada, and Australia. However, Indigenous use of archives in New Zealand rose dramatically through the 1990s and early 2000s.[34] Reconciliation in New Zealand is not separate from controlling and accessing records held in archives. An international meeting of Indigenous peoples' representatives in New Zealand in 1993 resulted in the Mataatua Declaration on Cultural and Intellectual Property Rights of Indigenous Peoples.[35] The Mataatua Declaration asks colonial institutions and agencies to repatriate Indigenous cultural objects to their traditional owners. The Declaration also demands that local, national, and international agencies recognize Indigenous nations and peoples as the stewards and guardians of their traditional knowledge with the right to protect and control the dissemination, access, and control of that knowledge.[36] Further, Māori academic and activist Ngahuia Te Awekotuku has developed a set of principles for researchers, and by extension archivists, based on the code of conduct for the New Zealand Association of Social Anthropologists that have been put into Māori cultural terms:

1. Aroha ki te tangata (a respect for people).
2. Kanohi kitea (the seen face, that is present yourself to people face to face).
3. Titiro, whakarongo . . . korero (look, listen . . . speak).
4. Manaaki ki te tangata (share and host people, be generous).
5. Kia tupato (be cautious).
6. Kaua e takahia te mana o te tangata (do not trample over the mana of people).
7. kia mahaki (don't flaunt your knowledge).[37]

This push for Indigenous access and control and movement away from Western knowledge systems in New Zealand, and internationally, has been moving toward a decolonial archival future for almost thirty years.

Decolonial archival interventions began across New Zealand, Australia, Canada, and the United States in the late twentieth century. International Indigenous communities communicated the importance of archival records in their revitalization and resistance. Taking back control over cultural and intellectual property was a key tenant in the 1993 draft of the United Nations Declaration on the Rights of Indigenous Peoples (UNDRIP) fourteen years before its final publication. Many of the articles of UNDRIP are relevant to Indigenous peoples' interventions in colonial archives and moving away from Western knowledge systems. Notably, articles 12 and 29 call to restore Indigenous control in archives and were created as a direct result of Māori input.[38] Article 12 recognizes the right to "the restitution of cultural, intellectual, religious and spiritual property taken without their free and informed consent or in violation of their laws, traditions and customs."[39] Article 29 extends to the ownership and control of Indigenous intellectual property held by institutions by stating that Indigenous peoples should receive the "recognition of the full ownership, control and protection of their cultural and intellectual property."[40]

We will explore the concept of community ownership and Indigenous intellectual property rights in chapter two, "Archives and Cultural Protocols." There will be a broader discussion about UNDRIP, archives, and protocols in chapter three, "Challenging Original Order and Provenance."

Moving Away from Colonial Archives

As the analysis in this chapter has illustrated, "Archives are social constructs. Their origins lie in the information needs and social values of the rulers, governments, businesses, associations, and individuals who establish and maintain them."[41] Archives are embedded in Western knowledge systems.[42] The way archives are constructed shapes the historian's understanding of the source and interpretations of the national heritage.[43] The shift from Western knowledge systems is debated as changing history, but history is not a fixed item from the past, and archival documents can be interpreted and organized in ways that tell different narratives of the same events. Debra Croswell has noted, "We are now our own authors, and we exercise the right of telling our own history."[44] Indigenous peoples have a right to access and tell their own history, and this means moving away from Western understandings of the past. Archives can be transformed to better suit Indigenous communities.

The archives contribute directly to Western systems of knowledge. They are a source for academic instruction, publishing, and public-facing heritage content. Trouillot has found that "[h]istorical narratives are premised on previous understandings, which are themselves premised on the distribution of archival power."[45] When archival organizations serve only to benefit the settler-colonial state and Western knowledge systems, they further contribute to academic scholarship's justification of one group's exploitation of another. The movement away from Western knowledge is therefore crucial to decolonization.[46] Using a decolonized approach to archives, one informed by Elders, land, and decolonization, allows for the archives to move beyond settler narratives.[47] We will further discuss decolonial archival interventions and moving away from Western knowledge systems in chapter five, "Indigenous Archival Futures."

NOTES

1. J. J. Ghaddar and Michelle Caswell, "'To Go Beyond': Towards a Decolonial Archival Praxis," *Archival Science* 19, no. 2 (2019): 75.
2. Aimee Carrillo Rowe and Eve Tuck, "Settler Colonialism and Cultural Studies: Ongoing Settlement, Cultural Production, and Resistance," *Cultural Studies ↔ Critical Methodologies* 17, no. 1 (2017): 3–13.

3. For more information about the Indian Act in Canada, see John F. Leslie, "The Indian Act: An Historical Perspective," *Canadian Parliamentary Review* 25, no. 2 (2002): 23–27.
4. Michel-Rolph Trouillot, *Silencing the Past: Power and the Production of History* (Boston, MA: Beacon Press, 2015): 5.
5. Elizabeth A. Povinelli, "The Woman on the Other Side of the Wall: Archiving the Otherwise in Postcolonial Digital Archives," *differences* 22, no. 1 (2011): 150–51.
6. Trouillot, *Silencing the Past*, 7.
7. Ghaddar and Caswell, "To Go Beyond," 76.
8. Ghaddar and Caswell, "To Go Beyond," 76.
9. National Archives and Records Administration, "About the National Archives of the United States," *National Archives and Records Administration*, accessed August 2, 2021, https://www.archives.gov/publications/general-info-leaflets/1-about-archives.html.
10. National Archives and Records Administration, "About the National Archives of the United States."
11. See National Archives and Records Administration, "American Indian Records in the National Archives," *National Archives and Records Administration*, https://www.archives.gov/research/native-americans.
12. National Archives and Records Administration, "American Indian Records in the National Archives," *National Archives and Records Administration*, https://www.archives.gov/research/native-americans.
13. National Archives and Records Administration, "Researching an Individual or Family," *National Archives and Records Administration*, https://www.archives.gov/research/native-americans/research-individual.
14. National Archives and Records Administration, "Researching an Individual or Family."
15. National Archives and Records Administration, "American Indian Records in the National Archives."
16. Laura L. Beebe, "Unsettling the Archive: Dis-Imagining Colonial Subjects to Re-Imagine Knowledge Production" (dissertation, University of California, San Diego, 2012): 5.
17. Beebe, "Unsettling the Archive," 5.
18. Audre Lorde, *Sister Outsider: Essays and Speeches* (Crossing Press, 2007), 123.
19. Ian E. Wilson, "'A Noble Dream': The Origins of the Public Archives of Canada," *Archivaria* 15 (January 1982): 16–17, https://archivaria.ca/index.php/archivaria/article/view/10966.
20. For more information on the Sixties Scoop, see Niigaanwewidam James Sinclair and Sharon Dainard, "Sixties Scoop," The Canadian Encyclopedia, Historica Canada, article published June 21, 2016; last edited November 13, 2020, https://www.thecanadianencyclopedia.ca/en/article/sixties-scoop.

21. J. J. Ghaddar, "The Spectre in the Archive: Truth, Reconciliation, and Indigenous Archival Memory," *Archivaria* 82, no. 1 (2016): 22.
22. Thomas P. Albritton, "The Myth of the Vanishing Race: Interpreting Historical Photographs of Native Americans" (master's thesis, Boise State University, 2021), 7.
23. Crystal Fraser and Zoe Todd, "Decolonial Sensibilities: Indigenous Research and Engaging with Archives in Contemporary Colonial Canada," *L'internationale* (2016), https://www.internationaleonline.org/research/decolonising_practices/54_decolonial_sensibilities_indigenous_research_and_engaging_with_archives_in_contemporary_colonial_canada, captured at https://perma.cc/LAL6-RJJJ.
24. National Archives of Australia, "Our History," https://www.naa.gov.au/about-us/our-organisation/our-history.
25. Natalie Harkin, "The Poetics of (Re)Mapping Archives: Memory in the Blood," *Journal of the Association for the Study of Australian Literature* 14, no. 3 (2014): 4.
26. The authors would like to note that Australia is not alone in this situation. Removal of children is an ongoing in the child welfare systems in Canada and the United States. In Canada there are currently more children in the child welfare system than at the height of the residential school policy. For more information on the child welfare system in Canada and its impacts on Indigenous peoples, see *Truth and Reconciliation Commission of Canada, What We Have Learned: Principles of Truth and Reconciliation* (2015): 109, https://ehprnh2mwo3.exactdn.com/wp-content/uploads/2021/01/Principles_English_Web.pdf, captured at https://perma.cc/C22B-ECY7.
27. Sue McKemmish, Shannon Faulkhead, and Lynette Russell, "Distrust in the Archive: Reconciling Records," *Archival Science* 11, no. 3–4 (2011): 219.
28. Peter Nagle and Richard Summerrell, *Aboriginal Deaths in Custody: The Royal Commission and Its Records, 1987–91* (Canberra, A.C.T.: Australian Archives, 2002).
29. National Archives of Australia, "Bringing Them Home Name Index," https://www.naa.gov.au/explore-collection/first-australians/bringing-them-home-name-index.
30. Evelyn Wareham, "'Our Own Identity, Our Own Taonga, Our Own Self Coming Back': Indigenous Voices in New Zealand Record-Keeping," *Archivaria* 52 (2001): 27, https://archivaria.ca/index.php/archivaria/article/view/12813.
31. Waitangi Tribunal, "About the Waitangi Tribunal," *Waitangi Tribunal,* https://waitangitribunal.govt.nz/about-waitangi-tribunal/past-present-future-of-waitangi-tribunal.
32. For more information about the makeup of the current iteration of the Waitangi Tribunal, see "About the Waitangi Tribunal," https://waitangitribunal.govt.nz/about-waitangi-tribunal/members-of-the-waitangi-tribunal.
33. Rachel Buchanan, "Decolonizing the Archives: The Work of New Zealand's Waitangi Tribunal," *Public History Review* 14 (2007): 45, https://doi.org/10.5130/phrj.v14i0.399.
34. Wareham, "Our Own Identity," 27.
35. Commission on Human Rights Submission of Discrimination and Protection of Minorities Working Group on Indigenous Peoples, the Mataatua Declaration on

Cultural and Intellectual Property Rights of Indigenous Peoples, July 1993, https://www.wipo.int/export/sites/www/tk/en/databases/creative_heritage/docs/mataatua.pdf, captured at https://perma.cc/6HQA-R48S.

36. Commission on Human Rights Submission.
37. Linda Tuhiwai Smith, *Decolonizing Methodologies: Research and Indigenous Peoples* (Otago, London and New York: Zed Books and Otago University Press, 1999): 136–37.
38. Wareham, "Our Own Identity," 27–29.
39. United Nations, Article 12, *Declaration on the Rights of Indigenous Peoples*, 2007. www.un.org/esa/socdev/unpfii/documents/DRIPS_en.pdf, captured at https://perma.cc/HRV8-4R36.
40. United Nations, Article UNDRIP. www.un.org/esa/socdev/unpfii/documents/DRIPS_en.pdf, captured at https://perma.cc/HRV8-4R36.
41. Joan M. Schwartz and Terry Cook, "Archives, Records, and Power: The Making of Modern Memory," *Archival Science* 2, no. 1 (2002): 3.
42. For more information on the connection of archives to Western knowledge systems, see Richard J. Cox "American Archival History: Its Development, Needs, and Opportunities," *American Archivist* 46, no. 1 (1983): 31–41, https://doi.org/10.17723/aarc.46.1.n43kl32721m250g1; Luciana Duranti, "The Archival Body of Knowledge: Archival Theory, Method, and Practice, and Graduate and Continuing Education," *Journal of Education for Library and Information Science* 34, no. 1 (1993): 8–24, https://doi.org/10.2307/40323707; Terry Cook, "'We Are What We Keep; We Keep What We Are': Archival Appraisal Past, Present and Future," *Journal of the Society of Archivists* 32, no. 2 (2011): 173–89, https://doi.org/10.1080/00379816.2011.619688.
43. Trouillot, *Silencing the Past*, 55.
44. Debra Croswell, "As Days Go By: An Introduction," in *Wiyaxayxt / Wiyaakaa'awn / As Days Go By Our History, Our Land, Our People*, edited by Jennifer Karson (Seattle: University of Washington Press, 2014), xv.
45. Trouillot, *Silencing the Past*, 55.
46. Tuhiwai Smith, *Decolonizing Methodologies*, 28–41.
47. Dallas Hunt, "Nikîkîwân 1: Contesting Settler Colonial Archives through Indigenous Oral History," *Canadian Literature* 230/231 (2016): 26.

2

Archives and Cultural Protocols

SETTLER-COLONIAL ARCHIVES CONTAIN VAST AMOUNTS OF INFORmation and records by and about Indigenous peoples.[1] The development of protocols to guide archival workers in the care and use of records about and by Indigenous peoples is not new or unique to any particular country. Indigenous communities and archival practitioners in the United States, Canada, Australia, and New Zealand have developed guidelines for the care of Indigenous archival materials. Likewise, the United Nations Declaration on the Rights of Indigenous Peoples (UNDRIP) offers guidance to archivists working with materials documenting the lives of Indigenous peoples. As Jane Anderson and Greg Younging have argued:

> Protocols provide guidelines for behaviour; they can function as a means for changing people's understanding of an issue and, thus, how they act in relation to it. In the context of the sharing, usage, and storage of Indigenous knowledge, protocols are being utilized as a strategic way of increasing reflective behaviour around Indigenous rights in cultural knowledge.[2]

Protocols can provide much-needed guidance to archives professionals on responding to Indigenous communities' needs and ethically forming relationships with Indigenous peoples. And each country's variation of a cultural stewardship protocol, along with the principles of UNDRIP, will impact the formation of policy, collection development, and arrangement and description.

UNDRIP and Archival Practice

In September 2007, the United Nations passed UNDRIP. The Declaration covers Indigenous self-determination, culture and language, health, education, land rights, and Indigenous law. In 2007, 143 nations voted in favor of UNDRIP, with only Canada, New Zealand, Australia, and the United States voting against the Declaration.[3] The four countries that voted against UNDRIP all have complex colonial histories and are rooted in settler nation-states with ongoing colonialism that continues to impact the lives of Indigenous peoples today.[4] Likewise, all four countries that voted against UNDRIP have archival systems deeply tied to colonialism and imperial power systems. Between 2009 and 2010, the four holdout countries signed on to the Declaration and since then have made varying levels of progress in implementing the recommendations of UNDRIP. Australia moved to adopt UNDRIP in 2009.[5] New Zealand followed by adopting the Declaration in 2010 and began developing a plan for measurable actions toward implementing UNDRIP in 2019.[6] The Government of Canada endorsed the Declaration in 2010 and, in 2020, introduced legislation to implement the Declaration in Canada.[7, 8] The United States announced its support for UNDRIP in December 2010.[9] It is important to note that not all Indigenous peoples feel that UNDRIP is the solution to reclaiming their rights. Kahnawá:ke scholar Gerald Taiaiake Alfred argues that colonialism must be addressed in "an Indigenous way according to Indigenous needs, values and principles."[10] A reliance on a colonial state's acceptance of Indigenous sovereignty creates a dependency on states to recognize rights, which makes documents like UNDRIP a further extension of colonial power and imperialism.

UNDRIP is not a legally binding document that requires states to make changes. However, it does offer a framework for cultural stewardship that can be a valuable starting point. This framework is directly applicable to archivists when considering records created by or documenting Indigenous peoples. UNDRIP articles 11, 12, and 31 relate to intellectual property, and these articles have direct ties to the intellectual property of archival materials. These articles all state that Indigenous peoples have the right to control and protect their own traditional culture and intellectual property.[11] Intellectual property includes materials held in archives. As Greg Bak has argued, "a number of UNDRIP articles emphasize the importance of Indigenous ownership and control overrepresentations of their own identity, culture and history. Although archives are not explicitly mentioned in UNDRIP, it is easy to see how archival missions are implicated."[12] UNDRIP articles 13 and 31 are further connected to the archival community. These articles assert: "Indigenous peoples have the right to maintain, control, protect, and develop their cultural heritage, traditional knowledge and traditional cultural expressions, as well as the manifestations of their sciences, technologies and cultures."[13] The Indigenous right "to maintain, control, protect, and develop" heritage and knowledge has significant ramifications for archival practice internationally. Archivists should think critically about the intellectual rights of Indigenous peoples to records that have long been attributed to government bodies and settlers. Likewise, archivists need to think about access to these records, particularly in relation to Indigenous concepts of property and privacy and the UNDRIP articles around intellectual property. While one of the fundamental principles of archival work is access, "the public domain has never been accommodating to [I]ndigenous models of knowledge production and circulation."[14] Indigenous traditional knowledge protocols often run contrary to the archival desire to make collections open to the public. Archivists need to acknowledge this fact and work with Indigenous communities to determine access and use policies based on UNDRIP and regional access protocols. Adhering to UNDRIP requires archives to shift away from colonial concepts of ownership and archival organization. UNDRIP pushes archives to think about ownership in terms of collective Indigenous community rights instead of the rights of individual creators. It requires rethinking archival practice from a decolonized lens and considering how Indigenous knowledge is represented in archives and how archives can be used for the benefit of relevant Indigenous communities. The cultural stewardship protocols from the United States, Canada, Australia, and New Zealand often include language that either mirrors UNDRIP or directly references UNDRIP and international concepts of Indigenous sovereignty and self-determination.

Protocols in the United States

The Protocols for Native American Archival Materials (PNAAM), established in 2007 by the First Archivist Circle, are an example of an effort to encourage respectful collaboration between Indigenous communities and archives. The First Archivist Circle membership that worked on PNAAM consisted of nineteen Indigenous and non-Indigenous archivists, museum workers, librarians, and others.[15] PNAAM includes specific recommendations for archival staff and organizations working with Indigenous archival material or Indigenous communities. Like UNDRIP, these protocols operate with the understanding that Indigenous communities are sovereign nations that have a right to govern their own cultural materials.[16]

PNAAM is divided into ten sections:

- Building Relationships of Mutual Respect
- Striving for Balance in Content and Perspectives
- Accessibility and Use
- Culturally Sensitive Materials
- Providing Context
- Native American Intellectual Property Issues
- Copying and Repatriation of Records to Native American Communities
- Native American Research Protocols
- Reciprocal Education and Training
- Awareness of Native American Communities and Issues

Each thematic section of PNAAM includes overarching themes followed by guidelines for actions. These guidelines are divided into actions for archives and libraries, and actions for Native American communities. The division of actions is reflective of PNAAM's relationship-based approach—none of the work proposed under PNAAM can be done without the participation of both archives professionals and Indigenous peoples. PNAAM covers a broad range of topics, including the importance of consulting with tribal communities when working with Native American archival materials, the importance of understanding and incorporating Native American values into archival practice, the need to rethink concepts of ownership and access in the context of Native American rights, and the need for care of culturally sensitive materials. PNAAM "advise[s] collecting institutions to acquire contemporary scholarship from the Indigenous perspective, to value both Native American and Western knowledge management systems, and to reexamine assumptions about existing archival practice."[17] Archivists and librarians are encouraged to seek a balance or compromise between Indigenous practices and Western systems of knowledge organization. This is something that takes ongoing work, and the foundation of PNAAM is the nation-to-nation relationships that Indigenous peoples hold in the United States and Canada, and an understanding that bridges need to be made between Indigenous and Eurocentric perspectives and practices.

However, PNAAM's recommendations were met with significant resistance, and they were not initially endorsed by the Society of American Archivists or the American Library Association. When PNAAM was released, many of the objections revolved around the destabilization of Western archival norms and the challenges they presented to colonial ethics, such as concepts of privacy, access, and ownership that are intertwined with archival practice.[18] This can feel uncomfortable to established colonial conventions because it presents a shift in the power dynamic and construction of the settler-colonial state narrative. Indeed, Stephanie Irlbacher-Fox has argued that "[u]sing, respecting, and making space for Indigenous Knowledge constitutes a fundamental challenge to power relations in whatever context it operates. Indigenous Knowledge has transformative potential with respect to confronting settler colonial norms within institutions in which it is used."[19] Shifting toward Indigenous-centered archival practice within a decolonized framework takes away power from colonial archives and power structures. This is a fundamental change in how archives operate. This change has been slow to happen, as evidenced by how long it took PNAAM to be endorsed and implemented in the United States.

In 2018, eleven years after PNAAM was released, the Society of American Archivists endorsed PNAAM as an external standard and recognized the protocols as "a foundation for archival practice in caring for culturally sensitive records" that "center Native American communities in the discussions of preservation and access to these materials."[20] This endorsement came after decisions in both 2008 and 2012 not to endorse the protocols and represents a renewed opportunity for archival practice in the United States to critically examine the care and use of Indigenous archival materials.[21] As of 2021, the Society of American Archivists (SAA), through its Native American Archives Section, maintains a page of information on PNAAM and has developed a series of case studies to see how PNAAM can be implemented in a range of organizational contexts.[22] These case studies include examples from organizations such as the American Philosophical Society (APS) and the Northern Arizona University's Cline Library. APS has created *Protocols for the Treatment of Indigenous Materials* following three years of collaboration between APS staff and a Native American Advisory Board.[23] The APS protocols are designed to determine which APS materials are culturally sensitive, assist with reproduction decisions relating to cultural materials, and support APS collaboration with Indigenous tribes.[24] In the case of the Cline Library, it was "one of the first national institutions to both endorse and adopt the *Protocols*."[25] In adopting the protocols, the Cline Library has used them to govern relationship building with Indigenous peoples and archival work, such as describing culturally sensitive materials, access decisions, and contextualizing archival records.[26] APS and the Cline Library are examples of organizations going beyond PNAAM and creating organizational-specific guidelines that support good relations with Indigenous communities and culturally sensitive stewardship of archival material. Beyond SAA and individual organizations like APS, the Association of College and Research Libraries (ACRL)—a division of the American Library Association—also endorsed PNAAM in 2020.[27, 28]

Protocols in Canada

Similar to the initial response to PNAAM, there was silence from archives professionals in Canada to the 1996 Report of the Royal Commission on Aboriginal Peoples (RCAP), which made specific recommendations for cultural heritage policies and best practices. The RCAP asserted that "correcting distortions of history are essential first steps in the process of healing between Aboriginal and non-Aboriginal people."[29] Likewise, RCAP Recommendation 3.6.4 explicitly calls for "museums and cultural institutions [to] adopt ethical guidelines governing all aspects of collection, disposition, display and interpretation of artifacts related to Aboriginal culture and heritage."[30] This section of the RCAP also advocates for Indigenous involvement in the development of policies and procedures at cultural heritage organizations, the creation and distribution of inventories that document holdings relevant to Indigenous peoples, and the necessity of ensuring that Indigenous communities have appropriate access and control over their heritage. Following the release of the RCAP, however, little was done at a political or professional association level to improve cross-cultural relationships or to increase access to Indigenous heritage held in archival repositories.

The 2015 final report of the Truth and Reconciliation Commission of Canada (TRC) reframes and restates many of the principles highlighted by RCAP in 1996. The TRC called on Canada's archives to work with Indigenous peoples to better present their cultures and histories, including histories of assimilation, cultural loss, and reclamation. The TRC has published clear recommendations for the archival and heritage professions in both its final report and its ninety-four Calls to Action. The TRC's final report argued: "Museums and archives, as sites of public memory and national history, have a key role to play in national reconciliation."[31] When the TRC released its Calls to Action, four directives explicitly addressed archives and museums in Canada, while several of the other calls contained content that could potentially impact archival practice. Call to Action no. 69 is directed at the operations of the Library and Archives Canada, requesting that it "fully adopt and implement the United Nations Declaration on the Rights of Indigenous Peoples and the United Nations Joinet-Orentlicher Principles, as related to Aboriginal people's inalienable right to know the truth about what happened and why, with regard to human rights violations committed against them in residential schools."[32] Beyond the Library and Archives Canada, Call to Action no. 70 requests "the federal government to provide the Canadian Association of Archivists to undertake, in collaboration with Aboriginal peoples, a national review of archival policies and best practices," with an emphasis on the archival community's compliance with UNDRIP and the United Nations Joinet-Orentlicher Principles (UNJOP).[33] This call links the UNDRIP and the UNJOP to the Indigenous right "to know the truth about what happened and why" relating to residential schools, but this practice could extend itself to other areas of forced assimilation and racist government policies under the Indian Act. One of the archival community's immediate reactions to Call to Action no. 70 was to note that the "Canadian Association of Archivists" mentioned in the call does not exist under that name. Is the call really referring to the Association of Canadian Archivists (ACA), the Canadian Council of Archives (CCA), or a completely new body for archives professionals? Ultimately, this work was picked up by the Steering Committee on Canada's Archives (SCCA), which includes membership from the ACA, the CCA, the Association des archivistes du Québec, the Council of Provincial and Territorial Archivists, and Library and Archives Canada.[34] Overall, the Calls to Action relating to archives request that archives professionals listen to, and work with, Indigenous communities. The calls are rooted in UNDRIP and UNJOP, and they require archivists to use these international principles as a framework for reconciliation.

The Steering Committee on Canada's Archives' Response to the Report of the Truth and Reconciliation Commission Taskforce (TRC-TF) has worked to create an action-based framework responding to the TRC. Established in 2016, the TRC-TF developed a number of deliverables for its work, including fostering community connections in the Canadian archival community and Indigenous communities in Canada, creating a multidisciplinary literature review relating to decolonial work in archives, developing protocols and principles for working with Indigenous communities, and designing a framework for reconciliation work in archives in Canada.[35] The work of the TRC-TF focused on Call to Action no. 70 and the creation of a set of recommendations for best approaches to reconciliation within the archives profession. Released in 2022, the *Reconciliation Framework: Response to the Report of the Truth and Reconciliation Commission Taskforce* is an actionable response based on six years of research into archival policies and best practices and is based on collaboration between settler archivists and Indigenous peoples. The framework is grounded in a vision statement that notes:

> This framework envisions a Canadian archival community that respects and supports First Nations, Inuit, and Métis sovereignty and self-determination and is committed to actively building equitable relationships with First Nations, Inuit, and Métis governments, communities, and

individuals. These relationships will recognize and uphold the inherent and inalienable rights of First Nations, Inuit, and Métis peoples to own, control, access, and possess their recorded memories, knowledge, information, and data.[36]

The vision statement for the framework is closely connected to UNDRIP, Indigenous sovereignty, and the right of Indigenous peoples to control their own records and archives. Like PNAAM, the Canadian framework is divided into several objects that represent different areas of relationships connected to archives and Indigenous peoples. The framework objectives include:

- Relationships of Respect, Responsibility, Relevance and Reciprocity
- Governance and Management Structures
- Professional Practice
- Ownership, Control and Possession
- Access
- Arrangement and Description
- Education

Each objective includes a goal, an overall summary, and actionable strategies to improve that objective. For example, the Professional Practice goal is noted as "The Canadian archival community must continue to build a body of professional practice that is committed to decolonization and reconciliation."[37] The actionable items connected to the Professional Practice goal include

1. Understand and acknowledge the colonial roots of mainstream archival theory, policies, and practice;
2. Encourage engagement by First Nations, Inuit, and Métis archivists, recordkeepers, and heritage professionals and practitioners in the activities of archival associations at the provincial/territorial, national, and international levels;
3. Provide training opportunities and support networks for trauma-informed archival practice; and
4. Support public education and advocacy led, informed, and undertaken by First Nations, Inuit, and Métis people.

Additionally, each actionable item includes examples of how each action can be achieved within the archival community. This emphasis on action is seen throughout the framework and is representative of the approach taken by the TRC-TF to actively respond to the TRC Calls to Action. Since its release in 2022, the framework has been endorsed by the Association of Canadian Archivists.[38] This early endorsement is a positive step toward the implementation and adoption of the framework across the Canadian archives profession. However, the implementation phase of this framework has just started, so it is difficult to compare to PNAAM or protocols from other countries, which have been in existence for decades. The authors are hopeful that Canadian archivists will take the framework to heart and engage with it in a meaningful way, resulting in real change to the archives profession.

Protocols in Australia

In the Australian context, the Aboriginal and Torres Strait Islander Protocols for Libraries, Archives and Information Services, which are endorsed by the Aboriginal and Torres Strait Islander Library, Information and Resource Network (ATSILIRN) and referred to as the ATSILIRN Protocols, act as cultural stewardship protocols for Indigenous library and archives materials. These protocols were originally released in 1995 by the Australian Library and Information Association. The most recent version of the protocols was released in 2012. The ATSILIRN Protocols are "intended to guide libraries, archives and information services in appropriate ways to interact with Aboriginal and Torres Strait Islander people in the communities which the organisations serve, and to handle materials with Aboriginal and Torres Strait Islander content."[39] They are designed as guidelines or frameworks for information professionals and are not meant to be a definitive source of information. The 2012 version of the protocols are divided into the following sections:

- Governance and management
- Content and perspectives
- Intellectual property
- Accessibility and use
- Description and classification
- Secret and sacred materials
- Offensive
- Staffing
- Developing professional practice
- Awareness of Aboriginal and Torres Strait Islander peoples and issues
- Copying and repatriation of records
- The digital environment

These sections are broadly framed within the idea that the protocols are a guide to good practice and should be interpreted on a case-by-case basis with each individual organization and Indigenous community. The protocols are not designed to be definitive; indeed, the protocols note, "It is unlikely they will cover all the issues you might face in your professional practice. However, they should provide you with a starting point for solving problems, and put you in touch with other practitioners who are working through similar scenarios."[40] The protocols are framed as guidelines for archival and library best practice. Like PNAAM and UNDRIP, the ATSILIRN Protocols are based on the fundamental rights of Indigenous peoples. For example, the governance and management section of the protocols notes that archivists and librarians are encouraged to "recognize Aboriginal and Torres Strait Islanders and the traditional owners and custodians of Australia."[41] This is the first protocol outlined in the ATSILIRN Protocols and provides a clear foundation for the remainder of the document by recognizing the inherent right of Indigenous peoples to their land and self-determination. This emphasis on the rights of Aboriginal and Torres Strait Islander peoples is further seen in the copyright section of the ATSILIRN Protocols, which calls on organizations to "[r]aise awareness of the issues surrounding cultural documentation and the need for cultural awareness training" and "develop ways, including the recognition of moral rights, to protect Aboriginal and Torres Strait Islander cultural and intellectual property."[42] UNDRIP clearly outlines Indigenous peoples as having intellectual property rights as well as moral rights over cultural knowledge and information. The copyright section in the ATSILIRN Protocols mirrors this and is another example of how the ATSILIRN Protocols reflect the fundamental rights of Indigenous peoples.

The development of the initial protocols decades before the TRC's Final Report and SAA endorsement of PNAAM provides an opportunity to examine long-term implementation of knowledge protocols and provide examples of ongoing Indigenous-driven information practices. In 2008—over a decade after the initial protocols were released—Alana Garwood-Houng and Fiona Blackburn found that few archival and library organizations reported on their implementation of the protocols, with any mentions of the protocols being mainly framed around endorsement not implementation.[43] In 2014, Garwood-Houng and Blackburn revisited their work and emphasized the need for more active uptake of the ATSILIRN Protocols. Their 2014 work highlights the ongoing relevance of the protocols and that they remain an excellent starting place for developing library and archival services for and about Aboriginal and Torres Strait Island people.[44] However, as Kirsten Thorpe has argued, "the adoption of protocols and guidelines in public libraries, archives, and cultural institutions has been ad hoc and their development not aligned with appropriate plans for action."[45] The ATSILIRN Protocols have been in existence for more than twenty-five years, however, they are still not uniformly applied or

Protocols in New Zealand

The last example of cultural protocols in this chapter looks at New Zealand and the rights of the Māori peoples. Māori rights in New Zealand are embedded in the Treaty of Waitangi, which was ratified in 1840 and 1860, and reaffirmed in 1975. The Treaty was signed in 1840 between the British Crown and approximately 540 Māori leaders. It is considered the founding document of New Zealand, and the treaty document confirmed British sovereignty over the country.[46] The Treaty has three articles; however, the interpretation of these articles varies depending on if the Treaty is read in English or Māori. In English, the Treaty's articles are interpreted as:

1. Establish British sovereignty over New Zealand.
2. Confirms the rights of Māori of their lands, forests, and fisheries, and other properties. But also gives the British Crown exclusive rights to the sale of these lands, forests, and fisheries.
3. Māori are 'given' the rights and privileges of British subjects and offered protection by the Queen of England.[47]

In Māori, these same articles are interpreted as:

1. The word *sovereignty* was translated as *kawanatanga* (meaning governance). There would have been no understanding of what the word sovereignty meant and the sacrifice it implied.
2. The phrase *other properties* was translated as *taonga* (meaning treasures). This refers to all material and nonmaterial heirlooms, including sacred lore, genealogies, and culture.
3. The word *protecting* is translated as *tikanga*. This translation implies that the Queen is allowing the protection of Māori peoples' customs.[48]

The Māori interpretation of the Treaty has significant implications for culture, heritage, and materials held in archival repositories. For example, the principle of *rangatiratanga* (chieftainship), found in the preamble to the Waitangi Treaty, asserts that Māori have control over their own customs and culture. This principle has been upheld through treaty litigation and legal cases brought to the Waitangi Tribunal.[49] The importance of the Treaty to archival practice is seen in how the New Zealand public archives are managed and the Public Records Act of 2005. Section 7 of the Public Records Act states:

Treaty of Waitangi (Te Tiriti o Waitangi)
In order to recognise and respect the Crown's responsibility to take appropriate account of the Treaty of Waitangi (Te Tiriti o Waitangi)—

(a) section 11 (which relates to the functions and duties of the Chief Archivist) requires the Chief Archivist to Archivist's functions, processes are in place for consulting with Māori; and
(b) section 14 (which relates to the establishment of the Archives Council) requires at least 2 members of the Archives Council to have a knowledge of tikanga Māori; and
(c) section 15 (which relates to the functions of the Archives Council) specifically recognises that the Archives Council may provide advice concerning recordkeeping and archive matters in which tikanga Māori is relevant; and
(d) section 26 (which relates to the approval of repositories) recognises that an iwi-based or hapu-based repository may be approved as a repository where public archives may be deposited for safekeeping.[50]

The Public Records Act enshrines a relationship between the Archives of New Zealand and the Māori people. It facilitates ongoing consultation and collaboration with Māori and encourages dialogue regarding the care and treatment of Māori archival materials. In addition to the Treaty of Waitangi, the 1993 Mataatua Declaration on Cultural and Intellectual Property Rights of Indigenous Peoples recognizes Māori as the caretakers of their cultural knowledge and as having control over that knowledge.[51] This declaration is aligned with the principles of UNDRIP and positions Māori peoples as in control of their own cultural and intellectual property. The fact that these rights have been enshrined in legal treaties as well as the Public Records Act is significant, providing cultural and intellectual property protection to Māori peoples under New Zealand law. However, beyond these legal documents, there is not an archives-specific protocol document similar to PNAAM or ATSILIRN in New Zealand. Some museums and cultural organizations have developed their own protocols for building relationships with the Māori people, however, this has not been uniformly implemented or codified by a professional body in New Zealand.

Protocols in Practice

Each of the four countries examined in this chapter—the United States, Canada, Australia, and New Zealand—has different protocols that reflect best practices for working with archival materials connected to Indigenous communities. These protocols represent work by Indigenous and non-Indigenous archivists, knowledge keepers, and community members to establish respectful relationships and respectful ways of engaging with Indigenous culture and history. New Zealand is the exception, with its relationship to Māori archival materials being defined through a treaty document and the Public Records Act. The other three countries' protocols are not currently codified by law and have seen mixed receptions, mixed uptake, and inconsistent application since their inception. The response to the protocols highlights the challenges associated with protocols, their lack of enforceability, and the need for implementation to be a core part of protocols. Despite these challenges, there are success stories in each country. There are archivists who have built reciprocal relationships with Indigenous communities and have embedded protocols in their processes and operations. For example, the Society of American Archivists has begun to highlight case studies of PNAAM implementation.[52] In Australia, the work of Garwood-Houng and Blackburn has continued to track the progress of the ATSILIRN protocols, showing both successful implementation and areas in need of improvement.[53] Implementation of the protocols requires trust building and establishing long-term relationships between organizations and Indigenous communities. However, "for institutions embarking on their first collaboration, relationship building can be challenging, particularly when the partners have different traditions and perspectives relating to specific rights and customs, such as those associated with access and use of cultural documentation."[54] A lot of work needs to go into implementing protocols more evenly across countries, and many more organizations need to consider how the protocols can inform their relationship building with Indigenous communities. These protocols have changed how archivists worldwide think about interacting with Indigenous communities and peoples. They provide a foundation for conversation and a foundation for building reciprocal relationships between archives and Indigenous communities. Indeed, the development of the three protocols from Australia, Canada, and the United States represent relationship-based work and are themselves the product of collaboration between archivists and Indigenous peoples. The protocols address practical, archival-specific concerns such as copyright, description, and access—areas not captured by broader overarching documents such as UNDRIP.

NOTES

1. Like chapter one, this chapter focuses on the colonial archives of Canada, the United States, Australia, and New Zealand. We decided to focus on these four countries based on their shared British colonial roots held by them, the English speaking nature of the countries, and the fact that all four countries had a similar response to the United Nations Declaration on the Rights of Indigenous Peoples (UNDRIP).
2. Jane Anderson and Greg Younging, "Renegotiated Relationships and New Understandings: Indigenous Protocols," in *Free Knowledge: Confronting the Commodification of Human Discovery*, edited by Patricia W. Elliot and Daryl H. Hepting (University of Regina Press, 2015), 180.
3. United Nations, "United Nations Declaration on the Rights of Indigenous Peoples," https://www.un.org/development/desa/indigenouspeoples/declaration-on-the-rights-of-indigenous-peoples.html.
4. For more information on settler nation-states and ongoing settler colonialism, see Eve Tuck and K. Wayne Yang, "Decolonization Is Not a Metaphor," *Decolonization: Indigeneity, Education & Society* 1, no. 1 (2012): 1–40.
5. Australian Human Rights Commission, "UN Declaration on the Rights of Indigenous Peoples," https://humanrights.gov.au/our-work/aboriginal-and-torres-strait-islander-social-justice/projects/un-declaration-rights.
6. Ministry of Māori Development, "UN Declaration on the Rights of Indigenous Peoples," https://www.tpk.govt.nz/en/whakamahia/un-declaration-on-the-rights-of-indigenous-peoples.
7. Indigenous and Northern Affairs Canada, "Canada's Statement of Support on the United Nations Declaration on the Rights of Indigenous Peoples," November 12, 2010, https://www.aadnc-aandc.gc.ca/eng/1309374239861/1309374546142.
8. Government of Canada, "Implementing the United Nations Declaration on the Rights of Indigenous Peoples in Canada," Government of Canada, 2021, https://www.justice.gc.ca/eng/declaration/index.html.
9. U.S. Department of State, "Announcement of U.S. Support for the United Nations Declaration on the Rights of Indigenous Peoples," January 12, 2011, https://2009-2017.state.gov/s/srgia/154553.htm.
10. Gerald Taiaiake Alfred, "Colonialism and State Dependency," *Journal of Aboriginal Health* 42 (November 2009): 48, https://jps.library.utoronto.ca/index.php/ijih/article/view/28982/23931.
11. United Nations, United Nations Declaration on the Rights of Indigenous Peoples, Resolution 61/295 adopted by the General Assembly 13 September 2007 (Geneva: United Nations, 2008), http://www.un.org/esa/socdev/unpfii/documents/DRIPS_en.pdf, captured at https://perma.cc/HRV8-4R36.
12. Greg Bak, "An Archival Overview of the TRC's Calls to Action," *Fonds d'Archives* 1 (2017): 4, https://fondsdarchives.ca/index.php/fondsdarchives/article/view/3/2.
13. United Nations, Declaration on the Rights of Indigenous Peoples.

14. Kimberly Christen, "Opening Archives: Respectful Repatriation," *American Archivist* 74, no. 1 (2011): 189, https://doi.org/10.17723/aarc.74.1.4233nv6nv6428521.
15. First Nations Circle, "Home," 2007, https://www2.nau.edu/libnap-p.
16. First Nations Circle, "Protocols for Native American Archival Materials," 2007, https://www2.nau.edu/libnap-p/protocols.html, captured at https://perma.cc/PUE2-F9ND.
17. Karen J. Underhill, "Protocols for Native American Archival Materials," *RBM: A Journal of Rare Books, Manuscripts, and Cultural Heritage* 7, no. 2 (2006): 138.
18. Frank Boles, David George-Shongo, and Christine Weideman, *Report: Task Force to Review Protocols for Native American Archival Materials* (Chicago: Society of American Archivists, 2008), 3–20, http://files.archivists.org/governance/taskforces/0208-NativeAmProtocols-IIIA.pdf, captured at https://perma.cc/ACJ5-CK6Q.
19. Stephanie Irlbacher-Fox, "Traditional Knowledge, Co-existence and Co-resistance," *Decolonization: Indigeneity, Education & Society* 3, no. 3 (2014): 148.
20. Society of American Archivists, "SAA Council Endorsement of Protocols of Native American Archival Materials," September 14, 2018, https://www2.archivists.org/statements/saa-council-endorsement-of-protocols-for-native-american-archival-materials, captured at https://perma.cc/J73S-W86R.
21. For more on the decade of debate within the American archival community around the PNAAM, see Kelsey Moen, "Moving Forward: Shifting Perspectives on the 'Protocols for Native American Archival Materials' in the Archives Community" (master's thesis, University of North Carolina at Chapel Hill, 2018), https://doi.org/10.17615/4kn3-y652.
22. See Society of American Archivists, "Access Policies for Native American Archival Materials—Case Studies," https://www2.archivists.org/publications/epubs/Native-American-Archival-Materials-Case-Studies.
23. American Philosophical Society, "The American Philosophical Society *Protocols for the Treatment of Indigenous Materials*," 2017, https://www.amphilsoc.org/sites/default/files/2017-11/attachments/APS%20Protocols.pdf, captured at https://perma.cc/ZS7Y-87DM.
24. American Philosophical Society, "The American Philosophical Society Protocols."
25. Jonathan Pringle, "Northern Arizona University's Cline Library and the Protocols," *Access Policies for Native American Archival Materials—Case Studies* (Chicago: Society of American Archivists, 2019): 3, https://www2.archivists.org/sites/all/files/Case_2_NAU_Cline_Library_and_Protocols.pdf, captured at https://perma.cc/38TV-DLPG.
26. Pringle, "Northern Arizona University's Cline Library and the Protocols."
27. David Free, "ACRL Endorses Protocols for Native American Materials," *ACRL Insider*, February 5, 2020, https://acrl.ala.org/acrlinsider/archives/19019.
28. A list of all endorsements of PNAAM can be found at https://www2.nau.edu/libnap-p/endorsements.html.

29. Royal Commission on Aboriginal Peoples (RCAP), *Report of the Royal Commission on Aboriginal Peoples*, vol. 5: Renewal: A Twenty-Year Commitment (Ottawa: Minister of Supply and Services Canada, 1996), 13.
30. RCAP, *Report of the Royal Commission*, 52.
31. Truth and Reconciliation Commission of Canada, *Canada's Residential Schools: Reconciliation: The Final Report of the Truth and Reconciliation Commission of Canada*, vol. 6 (Montreal and Kingston: McGill-Queen's University Press, 2015), 132.
32. Truth and Reconciliation Commission of Canada, "Calls to Action," 2015, https://ehprnh2mwo3.exactdn.com/wp-content/uploads/2021/01/Calls_to_Action_English2.pdf, captured at https://perma.cc/2KQC-AFDV.
33. United Nations Declaration on the Rights of Indigenous Peoples, ga Res 61/295, UNGAOR, 61st Sess, UN Doc a/res/61/295, 2007; United Nations, Economic and Social Council, Commission on Human Rights, Promotion and Protection of Human Rights, Impunity: Report of the Independent Expert to Update the Set of Principles to Combat Impunity, Diane Orentlicher, Addendum: Updated Set of Principles for the Protection and Promotion of Human Rights through Action to Combat Impunity, 61st Sess., Item 17 of the Provisional Agenda, Doc. e/cn.4/2005/102/, February 8, 2005, https://documents-dds-ny.un.org/doc/undoc/gen/g05/109/00/pdf/g0510900.pdf?OpenElement (UNJOP).
34. Steering Committee on Canada's Archives, "About Us," https://archives2026.com/about.
35. Erica Hernandez-Read, "SCCA – Response to the Report of the Truth and Reconciliation Commission Task Force (TRC-TF), Appendix E: Action Plan (v. 6)," Steering Committee on Canada's Archives, April 5, 2017, https://archives2026.files.wordpress.com/2017/05/2c-en-trc-action-plan-v-6_5-april-2017.pdf, captured at https://perma.cc/Z5JQ-VPN9.
36. Response to the Report of the Truth and Reconciliation Commission Taskforce of the Steering Committee on Canada's Archives, Reconciliation Framework: Response to the Report of the Truth and Reconciliation Commission Taskforce, 2022, https://archives2026.files.wordpress.com/2022/02/reconciliationframeworkreport_en.pdf, captured at https://perma.cc/2WGF-PXL4.
37. Response to the Report of the Truth and Reconciliation Commission Taskforce of the Steering Committee on Canada's Archives, Reconciliation Framework, 34.
38. Association of Canadian Archivists, "Reconciliation Framework: The Response to the Report of the Truth and Reconciliation Commission Taskforce," Archivists.ca, March 22, 2022, https://www.archivists.ca/Latest-News-Announcements/12676249.
39. Aboriginal and Torres Strait Islander Library, Information and Resource Network Inc., "The Protocols Are . . .," 2012, https://atsilirn.aiatsis.gov.au/protocols.php.
40. Aboriginal and Torres Strait Islander Library, Information and Resource Network Inc., "The Protocols Are Not . . .," 2012, https://atsilirn.aiatsis.gov.au/protocols.php.
41. Aboriginal and Torres Strait Islander Library, Information and Resource Network Inc., "Governance and Management," 2012, https://atsilirn.aiatsis.gov.au/protocols.php.

42. Aboriginal and Torres Strait Islander Library, Information and Resource Network Inc., "Intellectual Property," 2012, https://atsilirn.aiatsis.gov.au/protocols.php.
43. Alana Garwood-Houng and Fiona Blackburn, "Tracking the ATSILIRN Protocols: Maintaining the Focus on Indigenous Library Issues," Presentation at the Australian Library and Information Association Biennial Conference, Alice Springs, Australia, September 5, 2008.
44. Alana Garwood-Houng and Fiona Blackburn, "The ATSILIRN Protocols: A Twenty-First Century Guide to Appropriate Library Services for and about Aboriginal and Torres Strait Islander Peoples," *The Australian Library Journal* 63, no. 1 (2014): 4–15.
45. Kirsten Thorpe, "Transformative Praxis-Building Spaces for Indigenous Self-Determination in Libraries and Archives," *In the Library with the Lead Pipe*, 2019, https://www.inthelibrarywiththeleadpipe.org/2019/transformative-praxis.
46. The British Crown, "The Treaty of Waitangi, 1840," https://nzhistory.govt.nz/files/documents/treaty-kawharu-footnotes.pdf.
47. The British Crown, "The Treaty of Waitangi."
48. The British Crown, "The Treaty of Waitangi."
49. Evelyn Wareham, "'Our Own Identity, Our Own Taonga, Our Own Self Coming Back': Indigenous Voices in New Zealand Record-Keeping," *Archivaria* 52 (2001): 40.
50. Government of New Zealand, Section 7, Public Records Act, 2005, https://legislation.govt.nz/act/public/2005/0040/latest/DLM345713.html.
51. Commission on Human Rights Submission of Discrimination and Protection of Minorities Working Group on Indigenous Peoples, the Mataatua Declaration on Cultural and Intellectual Property Rights of Indigenous Peoples, July 1993, https://www.wipo.int/export/sites/www/tk/en/databases/creative_heritage/docs/mataatua.pdf, captured at https://perma.cc/6HQA-R48S.
52. Society of American Archivists, "Protocols for Native American Archival Materials: Information and Resources Page," https://www2.archivists.org/groups/native-american-archives-section/protocols-for-native-american-archival-materials-information-and-resources-page, captured at https://perma.cc/FYA9-BGER.
53. Garwood-Houng and Blackburn, "ATSILIRN," 4–15.
54. Elizabeth Joffrion and Natalia Fernández, "Collaborations between Tribal and Nontribal Organizations: Suggested Best Practices for Sharing Expertise, Cultural Resources, and Knowledge," *American Archivist* 78, no. 1 (2015): 193, https://doi.org/10.17723/0360-9081.78.1.192.

3

Challenging Original Order and Provenance

MANY ARCHIVES USE THE ARCHIVAL CONCEPT OF PROVENANCE TO inform how their archival materials are organized. The term *provenance* refers to the person or organization that created or collected the items in a fonds or collection. In practice, provenance is paired with the archival principle *respect des fonds*, which means that materials with the same provenance are kept together to preserve their context, history, and origin. Records that have different provenance are kept apart.[1] Provenance is further maintained through the archival principle of original order and the work of archivists to maintain the order in which materials were used. The colonial interpretation of archival provenance and original order can perpetuate extractive systems, which remove Indigenous knowledge from communities and is connected to the problem of archival organizations holding records about Indigenous communities without their consent or knowledge. Records documenting the lives of Indigenous peoples are often attributed to settlers, government agencies, and religious organizations. Archival provenance reinforces colonial understandings of history and ownership. This chapter will examine the ways in which provenance can be reimagined to meet the needs of Indigenous communities.

We agree with Livia Iacovino that a "[r]ecognition of Indigenous 'co-creatorship' or parallel provenance as an archival principle would be highly significant in providing evidence of claims in establishing Indigenous rights to records which capture their knowledge and identity."[2] Shifting the way we think about provenance has the potential to greatly impact Indigenous communities and access to archives that document the lives of Indigenous peoples around the world. Jeannette Allis Bastian has argued that:

> Archivists, as well as post-colonial scholars, have recognized the limitations of narrow interpretations and are testing the borders of provenance, looking beyond the physical record creator to discover context in place, in ethnicity and in collective memory in their efforts to fully embrace and interpret the record within a multi-cultural and boundaryless world.[3]

Our understanding of archival provenance needs to be expanded, stretched, and reinterpreted. This is particularly important when addressing records directly tied to colonialism and Indigenous communities. Provenance needs to be representative of relationships and power structures, and deeply consider how white supremacy impacts archival practices. We support incorporating what Tom Nesmith has termed *societal provenance*, which has the potential to allow for the understanding that records are not created in isolation and that they are often informed by more than one creator.[4] Records that document the lives of Indigenous peoples are often attributed to a single white creator or a single organizational entity. However, these records are often informed by Indigenous knowledge and Indigenous peoples. A societal approach to provenance that recognizes the role of Indigenous peoples as stewards of their own history and as cocreators of archival records provides a much more just, and culturally appropriate, form of provenance. Laura Millar has also argued for a broader understanding of provenance, suggesting that provenance should include information about who accumulated, used, stored, and managed records over time.[5] Millar has advocated specifically for the inclusion of creator(s) history, records history, and custodial history as part of provenance and sees provenance as layered and encompassing the history of archives.[6] Provenance can be expansive; it can include more than one creator and more than a single historical narrative. Post-custodial approaches to archives offer another example of pushing back against archival provenance. Speaking about a post-custodial paradigm, Christian Kelleher has argued,

> Archival principles such as provenance, order, custody, value, authenticity, and standardized systems of arrangement and description may fail to serve the interests of disadvantaged individuals and communities. When not critically tested, such principles have the potential to become agents of hegemony when they are doggedly, even unwittingly enforced by representatives of the dominant power.[7]

Postcustodial models represent a way of aggregating archival records based on community needs, decentering archival institutions and provenance. This approach offers opportunities for alternative arrangements, community-centered access, and collaborative approaches to archival practice. The Canadian examples in this chapter offer further insight into how post-custodial models can work in Indigenous contexts.

Cocreation and placing archival provenance back with Indigenous communities aligns with the United Nations Declaration on the Rights of Indigenous Peoples (UNDRIP), which states, "Indigenous peoples have the right to maintain, control, protect and develop their cultural heritage, traditional knowledge and traditional cultural expressions."[8] UNDRIP further calls on states to protect and ensure the rights of Indigenous peoples to govern their own cultural heritage and knowledge are respected and protected. The work of reframing archival provenance is part of a response to UNDRIP, an international call to acknowledge and ensure the rights of Indigenous peoples globally. As Jennifer Douglas has argued, "the archive would not exist without those who occupy it as subjects," and "when working with marginalized communities, the traditional definition of provenance is too narrow."[9] Indigenous peoples and their histories are part of many archives, and many archival holdings would not exist without Indigenous knowledge. Provenance needs to be expanded to acknowledge the role Indigenous peoples have played in shaping historical records, even if they are not the ones who are viewed as the "creators" under traditional understandings of archival provenance. The rest of this chapter outlines ways that archives have expanded thinking about archival provenance and original order. These case studies provide examples of community-focused provenance in practice.

Indigenous Provenance in the United States

The Karuk Tribe in the United States has been working since 2012 to establish the Sípnuuk Digital Library, Archives, and Museum. The name Sípnuuk comes from the Karuk word for storage basket, framing the digital archives as a place to store cultural heritage for the Karuk peoples.[10] The design of Sípnuuk was rooted in the needs and contexts of the Karuk Tribe to provide tribal oversight of cultural materials and Indigenous knowledge. The project is also founded on the principle that materials containing "Karuk traditional knowledge are the intellectual and cultural property of the Karuk People" and that these materials are made "available according to our Karuk cultural protocols regardless of their current copyright assignment."[11] This push against Western copyright is also seen in how Sípnuuk pushes back against archival principles of provenance and the ways in which materials are organized in the digital archives. Instead of being arranged by the creator or by where the materials come from, the website organizes information based on use and material type. Collections within Sípnuuk include community collections; video collection; how to, yafuseekyávans—cultural dressmakers; tribal culture; Frank Lake food collection; Karuk language; map collection; Karuk Holdings at the Field Museum; and a youth collection.[12] The organization of materials relates to Karuk community projects and community use, not where the materials came from or which colonial authority they might be attributed to. Many of the collections include a mixture of materials published by the United States Government, materials from other archives, and content created by Tribal members. Sípnuuk has been described as:

> . . . a Karuk-centered and decolonized space where knowledge can be accessed and shared through a self-representative lens in alignment with Karuk protocols and laws. It is positioned to correct the mistaken notion that non-Native repositories hold authoritative information about Karuk People and culture, to serve to educate the public and researchers about histories of colonial control over Karuk knowledge, and to provide guidance about authorized use of Karuk information.[13]

This tribal-centered repository shows the value of community-guided archival practice and how that can shift authority, challenge colonial conventions, and create new ways of organizing information that meets an Indigenous community's needs.

Similarly, the Carlisle Indian School Digital Resource Center uses a community-centered model to collect and make accessible archival records about the Carlisle Indian Industrial School. The Resource Center is an extensive database of Carlisle records, drawn from the National Archives and the Bureau of Indian Affairs papers and other sources.[14] The Resource Center has moved away from the original order and provenance of the materials, instead centering the former students in how materials are organized. For example, the Student Records section of the Center allows for records to be sorted in a range of ways, including date of entry to the school, document types, nations and tribes, and people.[15] This organization removes the records from their original colonial provenance and instead of privileging the administrators or government agency that would have created them, this organization is focused on the students. Additionally, the records are all keyword searchable, making it easier for family members to locate relatives who attended Carlisle. These same records are all part of the

National Archives and Records Administration (NARA), Records group 75. However, they are not nearly as accessible to the general public in their organization at NARA, and they don't have the same level of searchability on the NARA website. The Carlisle Center represents a community-centered approach to making Indian Boarding School records available and is an example of developing community-centered provenance.

Indigenous Provenance in Canada

Community-driven models of provenance are not a new concept. Many archives, museums, and libraries contain collections of ephemera, vertical files, or newspaper clippings, organized thematically. The general public frequently uses these collections to gain information about a specific topic or as a starting point for research. One option to move away from a hierarchical organization based on colonial ownership is to organize Indigenous archival records thematically like vertical files. For example, the National Centre for Truth and Reconciliation (NCTR) at the University of Manitoba and the University of British Columbia's Indian Residential School History and Dialogue Centre (IRSHDC), both located in Canada, have moved away from provenance-based organization. The NCTR and IRSHDC are post-custodial archives, with many of their records being digital reproductions of archival materials held by government and church organizations. Instead of organizing their records by which archives they came from or who created the records, the NCTR and IRSHDC organize their records based on residential schools. This allows users to easily navigate to records that interest them and allows people to search without knowing what church or branch of the Canadian government created particular records. This decenters the experience of the colonizer, those who created the records, and instead focuses on the archival users, Indigenous peoples. As well as moving away from traditional forms of provenance and original order, this method of organization prioritizes Survivor well-being. By decentering colonial structures, NCTR and IRSHDC limit how archives reflect colonial structures and potentially restrict the re-traumatization caused by archival research. Looking for archival records related to residential schools can be highly emotional and stressful. Having to navigate through church record systems, constantly seeing the names of church organizations and the names of residential school staff members, can create an additional burden to Survivors and intergenerational Survivors looking at archival records. By choosing not to present archival records in a colonial structure, the NCTR and IRSHDC are consciously choosing to support the needs of Indigenous peoples accessing the archives.

The NCTR and IRSHDC have also approached online access through visual navigation, and both organizations allow users to navigate records by accessing a map of residential schools. These maps allow users to center on a record from a school they are interested in without having to search multiple fonds or creators. Like the overall organization of the archives, this place-based organization centers the residential school and students' experiences on those schools, while making the creators of the records secondary. These are two examples of archives in Canada moving away from traditional concepts of provenance and supporting archival organization based on a thematic or placed-based arrangement that better supports information retrieval by Indigenous community members.

Beyond thematic or geographical-based organization, there is also potential for more engaged community provenance around archival arrangement. The Shingwauk Residential Schools Centre's (SRSC) approach to describing and naming archival collections is an example of shifting approaches to provenance based on feedback from Indigenous stakeholders. When McCracken began working at the SRSC in 2010, a collection of photographs connected to the Shingwauk Indian Residential School was known as the Principal's Collection. These photographs came from a range of undocumented sources and were divided into series based on the administration term of each Shingwauk principal. In this collection, about half of the photographs centered on the staff and principals of Shingwauk, with the other half of the photographs documenting Shingwauk students from 1900 to the 1960s. Organizing these photographs by the school principal forefronted the school administration's role in creating photographic documentation of the schools and used that information as the basis of provenance and arrangement. However, there was a significant downside to this arrangement—namely, that it centered on the staff of the Shingwauk School and not the students. At its most harmful, this resulted in more than one series named after principals who were known abusers, and anyone using those records would be repeatedly confronted with the abusers' names.

In 2015, McCracken, Hogan-Stacey, and SRSC staff began considering how these photographs could be better organized to meet the needs of the Survivor community that accessed the SRSC. Many Survivors and visitors to the SRSC wanted to search photographs by year, student name, or First Nation name. The use of Shingwauk principals' names as the description was not helping with access and was not making the photographs easier to find. SRSC staff worked closely with members of the Children of Shingwauk Alumni Association (CSAA)—comprised of Survivors and their descendants connected to the Shingwauk Indian Residential School—to get feedback on how they accessed photographs and what challenges they had in finding information in the SRSC archives. As a result of the discussion with Survivors, a decision was made to rename and reframe this collection. Instead of using the principal's tenure as the organizing provenance for the photographs, the photographs are now part of a Shingwauk Indian Residential School photograph collection and are organized by decade. The original arrangement of the photographs is included in a notes field. This renaming seems minor at first glance—but words have power, and how archival materials are described matters. By no longer centering the authority of the Shingwauk principals, this new organization prioritizes Survivor access and the needs of the SRSC users, not only Survivors who lived through the tenures of these principals, but now their descendants can also search for ancestors by year. This example highlights one of the ways that SRSC staff continue to approach arrangement and provenance through a community lens and guided by conversations with the Survivor community. However, it is also important to note that Indigenous communities are not homogenous and there can be varying opinions within a community. This can be the case within the CSAA. Sometimes, Survivors have different ideas about how archives should record their experiences. The CSAA operates through a sharing-circle consensus model, which means that decisions involve a lot of dialogue and reflection. The CSAA decided to rename the archival collections and reframe their organization through this style of governance. Through regular conversations and meetings with Survivors and their families, the SRSC has been able to take a community approach to archival arrangement and integrate Survivors' perspectives into their archival practice.

Indigenous Provenance in Australia

In Australia, the Australian Wumpurrarni-kari Archive was designed to use digital technology to provide Indigenous access to materials about the Warumungu peoples collected by colonial institutions, museums, and archives.[16] This project is an act of digital repatriation—it collects records from colonial sources and returns them to the community to be used in ways that the community sees fit. It leverages the search capacity of archives while prioritizing Warumungu protocols and knowledge systems in organizing information and deciding who is able to access materials.[17] This digital archives is an example of a project that has taken the structure of an archival system but redesigned it to fit the cultural protocol needs of an Indigenous community. Instead of using archival provenance to guide organization, the Wumpurrarni-kari Archive is governed by cultural protocols; materials are organized by what they mean within an Indigenous context and who should have access to the knowledge contained in the archives. Further, this digital project challenges how archives operate and how they are organized.[18] This project was the impetus for the creation of Mukurtu, an open-source content management system designed around the needs of Indigenous communities and cultural protocols. Further, "What the Warumungu community wanted was a platform whose functionality respected their dynamic social and cultural systems, relationships, and cultural protocols for sharing, circulating, and creating knowledge."[19] Mukurtu was created for the Wumpurrani-kari Archive because there was not a comparable content management system available that considered cultural protocols in the ways that were needed by the community. Its development is dependent on community input, particularly around how the platform would work, the interface, and its functionalities. Indeed, the Mukurtu development team noted that "the Mukurtu Wumpurrarni-kari archive (the safe keeping place belonging to the Warumungu people) was our first attempt to encode cultural protocols and social networks into the logic of the platform."[20] This archives represents a community-based digital archives focused on community protocols, shifting the conversation around ownership of archival materials. Many of the materials in the archives come from colonial sources—archives, organizations, and individuals. However, how the material is organized depends on their cultural context as dictated by the Warumungu community. Ownership and control over how material is organized is removed from colonial structures and instead relies upon Indigenous systems of knowledge. For example, some materials might only be available to women in the community because of cultural protocols.[21] This archives is an example of decolonizing and rethinking provenance, arrangement, and access. It reimagines the ways that archives are organized and shared, placing community access and protocol at the forefront.

Indigenous Provenance in New Zealand

The archival practice of the Te Reo o Taranaki has worked to return home the archival material of the Taranaki people. This process has involved disrupting archival provenance and has included partnering with mainstream archival repositories to digitally return archival records to community and disentangle records from institutional structures. For example, they worked with Archives New Zealand to "identify, digitise, and recontexualise catalogue metadata according to our defined fields."[22] Using the Mukurtu platform as a postcustodial archives, this allowed the Taranaki to gather records relating to the Taranaki Reo language, culture, lands, and heritage and describe them in a way that would be useful to community. The Taranaki undertook similar work to reclaim letters housed by the Alexander Turnbull Library known as the "Atkinson Letters."[23] In reclaiming these letters, the community was able to add additional metadata, context, and language resources that were useful to the Taranaki people. In both the case of the Archives New Zealand and Alexander Turnbull Library examples, the Taranaki peoples have asserted the need to rethink how these materials are arranged, described, and ordered. By digitally placing them in a Mukurtu database, the community has controlled the records outside of Western concepts of provenance and original order, and placed materials in contexts more useful for community.[24] Mukurtu focuses on community needs and is often used by Indigenous communities to organize records in ways that make sense to them. Mukurtu is a free, open-source system built within the Drupal content management system (CMS).[25] While Mukurtu aims to be an easy-to-access database, administered and managed by Indigenous communities, there is a need for someone to have an information management background and to understand the basics of server setup and web hosting. Often, an administrator account manages the Drupal interface for maintenance and troubleshooting purposes.[26] Once the community sets up a back-end structure, the community can fully customize how its database structure will work. Mukurtu operates with something called "the 3C's," which are communities, cultural protocols, and categories. Any Mukurtu database will need at least one community, one protocol, and one category to start adding digital heritage items to the CMS. The community can set individual user permissions, roles, and responsibilities to their database.[27] The idea is that every user and collaborator has a role, and responsibility reflects community practices.

Further, "the 3C's" allow for multiple understandings of digital heritage objects as communities can attach multiple cultural narratives, traditional knowledge, and diverse sets of protocols.[28] This structure is significant for nations with multiple tribes or ethnic groups living together in one community or for communities with items in their collections that only people who have undergone specific rites or ceremonies can access. Mukurtu is one example of disrupting colonial concepts of provenance and situating community understandings at the core of archival organization.

Another New Zealand example of shifting away from colonial understandings of provenance is the Tāmata Toiere digital repository, a project of Te Ipukarea—the National Māori Language Institute. This repository aims to provide information about *waiata* and *haka* (Māori song, chant, and dance).[29] Tāmata Toiere stores songs alongside lyrics, translation, historical information, biographical notes, and any cultural knowledge of the song. Songs are contextualized through a Māori lens, using a Māori understanding of culture. *Waiata* are also directly tied to language preservation, with language being essential for composing *waiata* and understanding the context of the *waiata*.[30] The repository contains historical, archival, and contemporary *waiata*, collecting *waiata* for future generations. The repository aims to:

- Preserve *waiata* and *haka* (especially compositions that have not been recorded elsewhere)
- Improve access of Māori to *waiata* and *haka*
- Provide a resource for learning and another means for Māori to "publish"
- Ensure Māori control of Māori knowledge.[31]

This repository pushed back against colonial provenance by organizing materials not based on where they may have been originally archived or recorded, but by genre, composer, and year. Many *waiata* are part of the public record of New Zealand, recorded as part of land court procedures or collected by government agents. Tāmata Toiere pushes back on government ownership and stewardship of this information, instead prioritizing community access and preservation for future generations of Māori peoples.

Digital Approaches to Provenance

The use of technology to reframe provenance and the original order is not limited to digital collections, and it is also possible to use digital technology to facilitate new arrangements for physical collections. For example, technology allows for the creation of multiple arrangements for the same records—archivists are not constrained by the physical box and how materials are ordered in that space. Instead, archivists can decide to arrange materials based on community needs and access concerns, which can be part of a larger ethical, community-driven approach to archival practice. This might mean that records are organized both chronologically and by geographic region. Likewise, the use of community-generated metadata tags or community-based description can facilitate searching records in a more thematic way.[32] This is not a new suggestion. In 2012, Jane Zhang undertook an extensive case study on the principle of original order in relation to digital archives, noting, "A digital archival system has the potential to enhance information discovery in archival records by enabling access options that the indirect access system of the traditional file structure model might not provide."[33] The use of digital technology can enhance the archival experience and provide archival users with a range of ways to access records beyond how they are physically organized. This arrangement can center the user and highlight relationships, interactions, timelines, geographic context, and other thematic commonalities between records. Linked data provides one option to highlight the relationships between digital records, however there are numerous ways that relationships between records can be expressed in digital spaces. This can include everything from hyperlinking to interoperable databases to the use of data visualizations.

The possibility of digital arrangement is particularly pertinent as many Indigenous communities look to use and arrange archival materials in their own ways, based on their own knowledge systems. Elizabeth Yakel has argued that "[a]rchivists should begin to think less in terms of a single, definitive, static arrangement and description process, but rather in terms of continuous, relative, fluid arrangements and descriptions. . . ."[34] Archival provenance and arrangement, particularly in a digital space, can be increasingly flexible, malleable, and adaptable to the needs of communities and archival users. An arrangement can change multiple times, and archives can organize collections in a myriad of ways that support Indigenous use of archival records. Archives cannot do this work in isolation. Rather, archives need to work with Indigenous communities to actively support their archival records and adapt to how Indigenous communities want to access and use archival materials. As Jeannette Allis Bastian has argued, "the content, context and structure of record creation is inextricably bound together in a vision of provenance and community that seeks, weighs and accommodates all the voices of a society by reimagining the many facets of its records as a synergistic and integral unit."[35] Records are much more complete and more contextualized when the community contributes to them. Platforms like Mukurtu have digital provenance with Indigenous contextualization, allowing communities to share and manage their own heritage.[36] Digitally being able to group records based on community needs is a powerful way to move away from colonial provenance. Societal provenance that is added by community adds layers of information to better understand archival materials. This context can also disrupt colonialism, giving a voice to Indigenous peoples who records are about but who may not have had a say in how the records were written or how they have been historically presented. This disruption is part of decolonial archival practice and part of challenging established historical narratives that have long privileged colonizers. Provenance and subsequent arrangement of archival materials is merely one part of archival practice that can be reimagined based on decolonial principles and the centering of Indigenous voices. The next chapter will take a closer look at how the archival practice of description can be challenged and changed as part of the larger picture of decolonizing and reinterpreting archival practice.

NOTES

1. For an in-depth look at the history and concept of archival provenance, see Jennifer Douglas, "Origins and Beyond: The Ongoing Evolution of Archival Ideas about Provenance," in *Currents of Archival Thinking*, edited by Heather MacNeil and Terry Eastwood, 2nd ed (Santa Barbara, CA: Libraries Unlimited, 2017): 25–52.
2. Livia Iacovino, "Rethinking Archival, Ethical and Legal Frameworks for Records of Indigenous Australian Communities: A Participant Relationship Model of Rights and Responsibilities," *Archival Science* 10, no. 4 (2010): 353–72.
3. Jeannette Allis Bastian, "Reading Colonial Records through an Archival Lens: The Provenance of Place, Space and Creation," *Archival Science* 6, no. 3–4 (2006): 281.
4. Tom Nesmith, "The Concept of Societal Provenance and Records of Nineteenth-Century Aboriginal–European Relations in Western Canada: Implications for Archival Theory and Practice," *Archival Science* 6, no. 3–4 (2006): 352.
5. Laura Millar, "The Death of the Fonds and the Resurrection of Provenance: Archival Context in Space and Time," *Archivaria* (2002): 1–15.
6. Millar, "The Death of the Fonds."
7. Christian Kelleher, "Archives Without Archives: (Re)Locating and (Re)Defining the Archive through Post-Custodial Praxis," *Journal of Critical Library and Information Studies* 1, no. 2 (2017): 17.
8. United Nations, Article 31, *Declaration on the Rights of Indigenous Peoples*, 2007, www.un.org/esa/socdev/unpfii/documents/DRIPS_en.pdf.
9. Douglas, "Origins and Beyond," 43.
10. Karuk Tribe, Lisa Hillman, Leaf Hillman, Adrienne R. S. Harling, Bari Talley, and Angela McLaughlin, "Building Sípnuuk: A Digital Library, Archives, and Museum for Indigenous Peoples," *Collection Management* 42, no. 3–4 (2017): 302, https://doi.org/10.1080/01462679.2017.1331870.
11. Karuk Tribe, "About," *Sípnuuk*, 2014, https://sipnuuk.karuk.us/about.
12. For more information, see https://sipnuuk.karuk.us/collections.
13. Karuk Tribe, Hillman, Hillman, Harling, Talley, and McLaughlin, "Building Sípnuuk," 312.
14. Carlisle Indian School Digital Resource Centre, "About," https://carlisleindian.dickinson.edu/page/about.
15. For more information, see https://carlisleindian.dickinson.edu/student_records.
16. This digital archives can be found at https://wumpurrarni-kari.libraries.wsu.edu.
17. Kimberly Christen, "Archival Challenges and Digital Solutions in Aboriginal Australia," *SAA Archaeological Recorder* 8, no. 2 (2008): 21–24.
18. Kimberly Christen, "Gone Digital: Aboriginal Remix and the Cultural Commons," *International Journal of Cultural Property* 12 (2005): 317.
19. Kimberly Christen, Alex Merrill, and Michael Wynne, "A Community of Relations: Mukurtu Hubs and Spokes," *D-Lib Magazine* 23, no. 5/6 (2017).
20. Christen, Merrill, and Wynne, "A Community of Relations."

21. For more information, see https://mukurtu.org/project/mukurtu-wumpurrarni-kari-archive.
22. Claire Hall, "Mukurtu for Mātauranga Māori: A Case Study in Indigenous Archiving for Reo and Tikanga Revitalisation," *Language, Culture & Technology* (2017): 193.
23. Hall, "Mukurtu for Mātauranga Māori," 195.
24. For more information on this community archives, see https://tereootaranaki.org/te-pute-routiriata.
25. Mukurtu, "What Is Mukurtu?," https://mukurtu.org/support/what-is-mukurtu.
26. Mukurtu, "Getting Started with Mukurtu CMS," https://mukurtu.org/support/getting-started-with-mukurtu-cms.
27. Mukurtu, "Getting Started."
28. Mukurtu, "About Mukurtu," https://mukurtu.org/about.
29. Visit the online repository at http://www.waiata.maori.nz.
30. Tāmata Toiere, "About This Site," Tāmata Toiere, http://www.waiata.maori.nz/en/about.
31. Rachael Ka'ai-Mahuta, "The Use of Digital Technology in the Preservation of Māori Song," *Te Kaharoa* 5, no. 1 (2012): 99–108.
32. See chapter four, "Community-Based Archival Description."
33. Jane Zhang, "Original Order in Digital Archives," *Archivaria* 74 (2012): 188.
34. Elizabeth Yakel, "Archival Representation," *Archival Science* 3, no. 1 (2003): 4.
35. Allis Bastian, "Reading Colonial Records through an Archival Lens," 269.
36. For more about Mukurtu, see https://mukurtu.org/about.

4

Community-Based Archival Description

INCREASED INVOLVEMENT OF INDIGENOUS COMMUNITIES IN ALL aspects of archival practice is part of decolonizing archival work and moving away from the colonial structures embedded in archival practice. Community-driven archival description acknowledges the vital role Indigenous peoples can play in contextualizing, reframing, and interpreting archival materials. Decolonized archival methods "counter normative approaches to research and information organization and create space for Indigenous peoples and local communities to engage in alternative approaches that reflect their own ontologies and epistemologies."[1] Decolonized archival practices require Indigenous communities to be actively involved in every aspect of archival practice—including description—with Indigenous peoples shaping conversations, policies, and ultimately archival practice itself. Archival description "is the process of capturing, collating, analysing, and organizing any information that serves to identify, manage, locate, and interpret the holdings of archival institutions and explain the contexts and records systems from which those holdings were selected."[2] Description is what makes archival records accessible and is what provides access points to archival materials. Descriptive practice involving communities is often referred to as participatory description or participatory archival practice. Anne J. Gilliland and Sue McKemmish have defined participatory archives and their work in a way that resonates with the authors' experience working with Indigenous communities. Gilliland and McKemmish have noted:

> Participatory archives acknowledge that multiple parties have rights, responsibilities, needs and perspectives with regard to the record. They are created by, for and with multiple communities, according to and respectful of community values, practices, beliefs and needs. Participatory archives offer a space for negotiating different perspectives, experiences and needs and a mechanism for reconciling the dual nature of archives that has been critiqued by scholars and distrusted by those who have been disenfranchised, silenced or otherwise marginalized or victimized by archives and recordkeeping more generally.[3]

Participatory archives are a shift in archival practice and in control over archival narratives. They remove the archivists as the central voice in archival practice and replace it with a collaborative approach to archiving. This is the type of participatory archival practice we are envisioning—a practice that includes Indigenous voices in multiple processes, conversations, and decision making. This practice is ongoing, rooted in relationships, and can take the shape of project-specific description work or ongoing archival descriptive practices. It is important to note that description is never neutral. Often archival description is shaped by the knowledge of a single archivist and that archivist's positionality. Opening archival description to be more participatory is decentering the power of the archivist—it changes the lens through which description happens. Lauren Haberstock has argued that "[p]articipatory description should not be an extractive process, but rather should be a relationship-driven process that works to build community ownership of archival records."[4] Participatory description should not create added labor for communities; it should be framed based on Indigenous community priorities and needs.

There are numerous ways that participatory description can unfold in collaboration with Indigenous communities. It might look like involving Indigenous peoples in description as soon as records are donated, or it might look like redescription projects focused on recontextualizing archival records. Participatory description could involve Elders, knowledge holders, youth, and other Indigenous community members. Haberstock has further suggested that decolonized methodologies have a place in archival description and present new opportunities for archivists looking to work with Indigenous communities,

> the emphasis on storytelling and the power of language present in decolonizing methodologies empower archivists engaged in participatory approaches to listen, to seek out the multitudinous facets that construct a narrative, and to critically examine the terminology used in the archives.

Is space given for the contextualization and explanation of an object's use? What web of relationships needs to be in place in order to properly situate an artifact?[5]

Participatory description can look like having conversations with communities represented in archival collections. Description can be more interactive than any single archivist deciding how to associate metadata with materials. Indeed, it can be an active process, involving community, Elders, and knowledge holders. This process can be done for records that have yet to be described and for records that have been previously described. Livia Iacovino has argued that "[r]etrospectively reshaping the archive to allow for individuals and groups to have their voices heard either through digital annotations or a virtual community space would be of specific benefit to minorities and Indigenous groups as records were often tools of or witnesses to discrimination in many countries."[6] Redescription and the activation of records by Indigenous communities can change the meaning of records and create community connections to archives. It is important to remember that not every Indigenous community will want to approach working with archives or description from the same lens or through the same process. There is not a one-size-fits-all answer to participatory archives or participatory description. Belinda Battley has suggested that archivists engaging in community, working with community records, need to answer several questions before they proceed, including, "How can the process be inclusive and transparent for the community? How to best get to know and work with the community? Are there people who can be connectors and advisors? What cultural practices to take into account? How does this community use records in maintaining its collective memory? What skills and knowledge already exist in the community that are helping maintain recordkeeping processes?"[7] These questions are just the beginning to learn about community and how to situate archives in relation to community groups. A lot of preparatory work is required before engaging with a community and community archival practice. Much of this work centers around understanding the community, getting to know community members, and building relationships. This work is going to look different in each community context. The case study examples demonstrate what has worked at specific archives with specific Indigenous communities and should not be considered the only options of how participatory description can work. Rather, these examples should be looked at as models and considered when working to build a participatory description practice in collaboration with community.

American Participatory Description and Community Archives

This section examines the American Philosophical Society (APS) Library, located in Philadelphia, Pennsylvania, in the United States. The APS "is the oldest repository in North America of archival materials on the languages, cultures, and continuing presence of Indigenous peoples of the Americas . . . the collections now consist of about 1,900 linear feet of manuscripts, photographs, and audiovisual materials relating to more than 650 Indigenous cultures of the Americas, dating from 1553 to 2017."[8] Many of the archival materials held by the APS were collected by non-Indigenous peoples and removed from the context and care of their respective Indigenous communities. In 2007, the APS started several projects related to its Indigenous collections, focusing on increased access and cultural awareness. These projects included the development of the Center for Native American and Indigenous Research (CNAIR) at APS and the creation of the Digital Knowledge Sharing project.[9] The APS Digital Knowledge Sharing project is founded on the values of community-based scholarship, which is based on ideals similar to that of participatory archiving. Namely, community-based scholarship is founded on respectful, reciprocal collaboration guided by community. Timothy B. Powell, who worked as the first director of CNAIR, has argued that "the success of community-based scholarship depends on reimagining the relationships between academic knowledge systems and the knowledge systems maintained by traditional knowledge keepers and community members."[10] Community engagement can transform knowledge systems, including archival systems. In the case of the APS and the Digital Knowledge Sharing project, community engagement has reconnected Indigenous nations and families with documents, history, and culture that had been removed from their communities for hundreds of years. It has also contributed to the integration of Indigenous knowledge into the archival record and a much more robust understanding of the Indigenous materials produced at APS. For example, partnerships developed under the Digital Knowledge Sharing project have resulted in the integration of Indigenous language into archival description. This has included updating Indigenous community place names based on knowledge provided by language speakers. Likewise, the names of Indigenous peoples who cocreated archival materials are now actively and prominently documented when that information is known.[11]

Canadian Participatory Description and Community Archives

One Canadian example of participatory description can be found in the work of the Shingwauk Residential Schools Centre (SRSC), located in Sault Ste. Marie, Ontario, Canada. As mentioned in the introduction of this book, both authors have worked in the SRSC and have ties to the Children of Shingwauk Alumni Association (CSAA). This example draws on the professional and personal experiences of McCracken and Hogan-Stacey. Since its establishment in the 1980s, one of the main goals of the SRSC has been to increase the accessibility of residential school documents and photographs to Indigenous community members. Historically, residential school photographs were used to justify the need for and to celebrate the perceived success of the residential school system. Residential school photographs belonged to and were predominantly created by school administrators and staff.[12] Many Survivors of the residential school system are named or pictured in residential school records, however, very few Survivors or families hold copies of these materials.[13] The longest-running SRSC project that responds to the need for community access is the Remember the Children: Photo Identification Project, which started in 2005. This photo identification project represents not only a form of access but a form of participatory description.[14] The aims of Remember the Children are to connect Survivors and communities with photographs of residential schools and to involve community members in identifying and describing the photographs.

The project has created reproduction photo albums for the eighteen federally recognized residential schools in Ontario, Canada, as well as photo albums for a select number of residential schools from other provinces in Canada. These photo albums have been shared at community events with Survivors and family members. They serve as a starting point of dialogue within families and communities, and also with the archives. Community members have been invited to write on the reproduction albums any names, context, and anything they recall connected to photographs in the albums. The foundation of this project—adding names to photographs—seems small at first glance. However, adding names to archival photographs can have a profound impact on the individuals, families, and communities that have been directly affected by the residential school system and has equally important effects on broader society. It has been noted that "this act of matching names to photographs in the process of archivization is seemingly small and simple, it has had an overwhelming impact on countering societal silences."[15] The Remember the Children project is community-engaged description, approached in a way that is meaningful to the Survivor community.

Photographs were the most requested type of archival materials by Survivors and community members at the SRSC. When SRSC staff add names, context, or other information to the reproduction photo albums, they transfer this information back to the archival record, connecting community outreach to archival description and archival practice. Community members are also encouraged to ask for copies of photos, which the SRSC provides free of charge as part of this project. Remember the Children has been successful because community needs drive it, it works with the community, and it places archival practice as secondary. The most important part of the project is sharing the photographs with those who are connected to them. The added names and context of the photographs are important—but SRSC staff aren't demanding that information. Rather, it is collected passively and in a way that emphasizes community members feeling comfortable sharing information. Archival records relating to residential schools are not just records documenting administrative perspectives on residential schools; they are also records of Indigenous experiences, lives lived, and generations that have passed on. Archival records can be part of the collective memory of Indigenous communities and families. When photographs are described with the proper names attached, family members can search for their names with the appropriate spelling and retrieve records that are relevant to their needs. Future generations and descendants will not have to look through hundreds of photos hoping to recognize an ancestor they may never have seen. It can also link photographic records to administrative records and help tell more complete stories for those using the collections. A single photograph or a single line in an attendance register can fill in family trees and result in adding new information to subsequent generations' narratives. It is an example of the large amount of power the archives hold in colonized lives. A small piece of information can significantly impact families searching for answers, and community archival spaces can aid in healing journeys.

Another Canadian example is the Aanischaaukamikw Cree Cultural Institute (ACCI), developed in collaboration with all nine communities in Eeyou Istchee, a territory represented by the Grand Council of the Crees. Located in Oujé Bougoumou, Quebec, Canada, ACCI was founded with the understanding that "Cree culture must be captured, maintained, shared, celebrated, and practiced" and that there is a "need for a central place for the protection of 'the ways,' and has developed a vision for Aanischaaukamikw over several decades."[16] ACCI has worked to physically and digitally repatriate material culture and archival collections connected to the Eeyou Istchee community, so community members do not need to travel to Library and Archives Canada or other government institutions to research their own history. Annie Bosum and Ashley Dunne (2017) have reflected on ACCI as "the gateway where traditional knowledge and culture are documented and shared with our communities and the world. Old and new ways of Cree life are showcased for all who visit, celebrating the uniqueness, elegance, and diversity of our culture."[17] ACCI is an example of complete Indigenous ownership and management of regional cultural heritage and activities. ACCI is a space and archives that reflect Indigenous sovereignty, ownership, intellectual property, and governance while caring for both historical and contemporary traditions and teachings. This archives embodies community participation in management, governance, and administration. They are embracing self-determination and the rights of Indigenous peoples to decide how their histories, cultures, and information are shared, owned, presented, and accessed. The archives is often embedded in the fabric of communities, part of community healing efforts, and part of ongoing culture and language reclamation.

Australian Participatory Description and Community Archives

The next example looks at the Aboriginal and Torres Strait Islander Data Archive (ATSIDA) and the work of ATSIDA around cocreation and community-based archival description. ATSIDA "provides a trusted, secure digital repository for the long term preservation of and access to research about Indigenous Australians."[18] It is a thematic archives tied to the Australian Data Archive and is a partnership between the Australian National University, the University of Melbourne, the University of Western Australia, and the University of Queensland.[19] ATSIDA contains research datasets created by a range of scholars connected to Aboriginal and Torres Strait Islander communities. The project has a commitment to repatriating the information collected in ATSIDA to the Indigenous peoples it relates to. In practice, it means that:

> ATSIDA seeks to ensure the return of knowledge documented in research projects to the relevant Indigenous communities. Researchers are requested to identify materials from their full datasets to be returned to a relevant community keeping place. It may be that all of the material is appropriate for return. . . . Alternatively, only a small portion of material may be returned due to privacy, confidentiality or cultural reasons. This is determined jointly by the researcher and community members.[20]

A lot of the work ATSIDA does is around repatriation. However, it is also concerned with how research and information are presented and described. Anne J. Gilliland has noted ATSIDA is a data archives that "supports forms of descriptive access that moves it beyond conventional archival approaches, including item and within-item access, multiple arrangements and presentation schemes, and community annotation capabilities."[21] The annotation capability of ATSIDA is a form of community description and redescription of archival materials. Part of redescribing archives from an Indigenous lens includes the ability to speak back to archives and identify what information is important to individuals and communities. Indigenous communities should have "the right to respond to, update, query or comment on data held in the archive."[22] ATSIDA is an example of the ways that records can forefront the needs of Indigenous communities, with the forms of archives and archival descriptions being reimagined based on the needs of the community. ATSIDA is governed by a set of protocols that guide work with Indigenous communities. The protocols have three core principles: respect, trust, and engagement.[23] These three principles emphasize that Aboriginal and Torres Strait Islander peoples, cultures, and protocols are to be respected and that strong relationships should be made between communities and collecting institutions. The protocols also highlight the importance of the return of Indigenous knowledge documented in research projects and the ownership of Indigenous knowledge by community. The importance of ATSIDA's approach to records and its involvement of Indigenous communities have been noted by Gilliland, who argues that:

> ATSIDA illustrates the ways in which the same records with alternate culturally and situationally appropriate metadata, including community-supplied annotations (increasingly via social media), when managed in accordance with Indigenous needs, concerns, and beliefs, and with professional awareness of the urgency that is often involved, can support redress for that violence and the reconstruction of identity, memory, and lives.[24]

Archives and records about Indigenous peoples have the potential to change lives. They can inform community knowledge, family knowledge, and knowledge about personal histories. In many countries, Indigenous ceremonies and cultural practices have been prohibited by law.

Archival records are also important for those who have lost generational knowledge due to relocation or policies of forced removal. Archives that hold census records, records from industrial or residential schools, and government department documents can be vital for those who are reconnecting to their families or communities. Finding their parents, grandparents, or great-grandparents can help those who were adopted out to non-Indigenous families or forcibly removed from their traditional territory. Whether Indigenous peoples and communities want to reclaim traditional practices or understand their own familial histories, archives need to be structured in ways that make this process easier, not more difficult.

In addition to ATSIDA, the Koorie Heritage Archive (KHA) and the Koorie Archiving System, which was developed out of the Trust and Technology Project with the Koorie Heritage Trust Inc., is an example of an Indigenous archives situated in Australia that is actively engaged with Indigenous identity in the present.[25] Kooramyee Cooper and Sharon Huebner have noted, "The KHA plays a fundamental part in working out who we are. It helps rebuild oral histories; kinship laws; cultural handing down of past lores; dances; languages. It allows Koorie people and community in Victoria, to preserve who they are, in their own way."[26] This community-centered archives uses digital technology to make materials connected to Koorie peoples more accessible. This is accomplished through creating a rich media library for community members and a digital space in which Koorie users and community members can provide their own perspectives, context, and knowledge on government records about the community. The archives is evolving and is based on participatory archiving principles that allow Koorie people to contribute to describing materials and determining the access protocols of materials. Cooper and Huebner further describe the KHA, noting that "it empowers Koorie people; it encourages them to record; to take ownership of who they are; and what place they play in our community. Young or old, everyone plays a part, and the KHA allows that."[27] The KHA is an intergenerational archives that stretches into the past and into the future, facilitating information sharing from Elders to youth; it is dynamic in its ability to reach community. The KHA is an archive that allows community members to preserve their history in a way that seems appropriate to them, not in a way that is dictated by colonial archival structures. Additionally, the Koorie Archiving System proposed including the ability for Indigenous community members to provide "annotations that interpret, correct, or provide context for information sourced from official records."[28] This would provide a space for reply, speaking back to colonial records and reinterpreting them based on Koorie knowledge and worldviews—something that isn't easily achieved in colonial archiving systems. The KHA and the Koorie Archiving System technology is an example of an Indigenous-centered digital archives space that is driven by community needs. This dynamic digital space pushes the boundaries of archives and allows for Indigenous peoples to document their history and present on their terms.

New Zealand Participatory Description and Community Archives

The National Library of New Zealand, also known as Te Puna Mātauranga o Aotearoa, was established in 1965 under the National Library Act, which brought together the General Assembly Library, the Alexander Turnbull Library, and the National Library Service.[29] The Alexander Turnbull Library includes unpublished material relating to Māori peoples, including "manuscripts; drawings, paintings and prints; ephemera; cartography; oral history; and photography."[30] The National Library has worked to build relationships with the Māori people and maintains principles for the care and preservation of Māori materials. This care is rooted in four principles tied to the Treaty of Waitangi:[31]

- Kaitaiakitanga | Guardianship
- Te mahi tahitanga | Relationships
- Te whakaatu i ngā kōrero mō te kaituhi | Attribution
- Te whakapakari i ngā kaimahi | Cultural development[32]

The Treaty of Waitangi is a foundational document that guides the relationship between the Crown in New Zealand and Māori peoples. The Treaty has specific promises to protect Māori culture, which have informed the work of the National Library.[33] In connecting to the concept of archival description and participatory archives, the National Library notes that it "seeks collaborative relationships with families and descent groups connected to taonga in its collections. These relationships are drawn on to make decisions about all aspects of the management of these items, including conservation, exhibition and attribution regardless of whether the Library is legally the owner or guardian of the item in the collection."[34] The document also goes on to indicate that it is the responsibility of the National Library to develop effective relationships with the Māori people to guide its practices. Bradford W. Morse has argued that "[t]he incorporation of mātauranga Māori concepts and values is an acknowledgement by the National Library that Māori are the primary holders of this traditional knowledge and wisdom."[35] This acknowledgment is also seen through the inclusion of Māori specialists who work to help "the ancestral voices speak" within the archival collections held at the Turnbull.[36]

On the description side, the Māori Subject Headings Project is an example of descriptions that actively engage community knowledge. The Subject Headings Project has included the development of the Iwi Hapū Names List, an evolving list documenting iwi and hapū names. The project has also included the development of the Ngā Ūpoko Tukutuk, or Māori Subject Headings, which are designed to create ways for catalogers and archivists to describe materials related to Māori. These subject headings include "a Māori worldview in its construction, in that terms are woven into a wharenui (meeting house) structure. The thesaurus recognises the relationships between te taha tinana (the people), te taha wairua (the spiritual) and te taha hinengaro (the mind). It incorporates Māori ways of thinking and te reo Māori into an information retrieval model."[37] Māori ways of thinking are also known as Mātauranga Māori, or ways of being engaged in the world. This way of thinking uses cultural practices and principles to understand the world.[38] This digital portal allows archivists and librarians to search for standardized terms in te reo Māori, which can then be used when describing content.[39] Ngā Ūpoko Tukutuk provides a structured path system to Māori worldview, within the context of archives and libraries, and is an example of descriptive practices using Indigenous worldview. Indigenous ways of knowing and understanding are being integrated into policy, practice, and description at the National Library, and more specifically in the Turnbull collections, which contain vast amounts of information related to the Māori.

Beyond the Turnbull collections, the Pei Te Hurinui Jones collection held at the University of Waikato is another Māori-centered archival collection that has been cared for using Indigenous community guidance and culture. The collection includes eighty boxes of textual records and photographs relating to the life and work of Pei Jones, who lived from 1898–1976.[40] When processing the collection, "the entire collection and each *taonga* was considered in terms of its cultural values and spiritual connection to Pei Jones."[41] The archival materials were treated as cultural treasures, cultural knowledge, and as having spiritual elements. The records are not merely paper; they are embodiments of culture. The involvement of community is further seen in the collection room. Known as *Mahi Māreikura*, this room is used to store and display the *taonga* connected to Pei Te Hurinui Jones.[42] Creating a culturally appropriate storage space for the care of archival materials is decolonizing work. It is rethinking how archives are cared for, described, and housed. Further, when working with the Pei Te Hurinui Jones collection, university staff used *tikanga* (protocols and custom) to guide their decision-making process, and archival processes were considered in relation to *mana*, *whakapapa* (genealogy), and *kōrero* (history).[43] The Pei Te Hurinui Jones collection is an example of Western archival practices, including description, being decentered. Instead, workflow and how archival materials are managed is guided by cultural and spiritual practices.

Approaching Decolonizing Description

As the case studies demonstrate, what participatory archival description looks like can vary greatly. It can involve going into a community, working with language speakers, annotating records, or creating robust tools to help describe archival materials. It can also include reparative descriptive practices, an archival practice that actively addresses racism and harms found in records. Mainstream archives have often used oppressive, racist, or misrepresentative language within archival description. Actively redescribing these records can be part of participatory description, shifting power dynamics away from the archivist and focusing on community needs. It means pushing back against the narrative that archives are neutral, calling out oppressive archival practices, and working with community to understand the best way to describe community.[44] Redescription is one way to do participatory archival description, but there is not a single right way to do it. Rather, what this form of participatory work looks like should be informed by the Indigenous community, relationship building, and ongoing conversations. With the need for community-informed practices in mind, the authors recommend the following approaches to decolonizing description:

1. Participatory description should not add additional burdens to Indigenous communities. Rather it should be driven by community engagement and needs.[45] It is never too late to begin a participatory description project. Records that were described decades ago can be redescribed and used to facilitate ongoing communication with Indigenous communities.
2. Relationship building needs to come first. Description work and redescription work are not going to be done quickly and need to be based in respectful relationships with Indigenous communities.
3. Work with Indigenous communities to determine the best approach to description. This might look like annotation, keyword building, adding names to photographs, or writing descriptions from scratch. All of these (and other) approaches are valid.
4. Descriptive practices and collaboration should respect the sovereignty of Indigenous nations and their inherent right to control their own information.

This is work. Many archivists, particularly in small archives, are overburdened already. We argue that archivists need to shift priorities and advocate for the importance of relationship building and decolonial archival practice. This may mean leaning on professional standards such as PNAAM or other cultural protocols to show administrators the importance of this work. It may mean seeking additional funding to support community outreach and relationship building. These suggestions are not definitive. Instead, they are a starting point for archivists and archival organizations working to reimagine descriptive practices in decolonial ways.

NOTES

1. Lauren Haberstock, "Participatory Description: Decolonizing Descriptive Methodologies in Archives," *Archival Science* 20, no. 2 (2020): 130.
2. Victoria Irons Walch, "Introduction," in *Standards for Archival Description: A Handbook* (Chicago: Society of American Archivists, 1994), http://www.archivists.org/catalog/stds99/intro.html, captured at https://perma.cc/Y3CM-KWX8.
3. Anne J. Gilliland and Sue McKemmish, "The Role of Participatory Archives in Furthering Human Rights, Reconciliation and Recovery," *Atlanti: Review for Modern Archival Theory and Practice* 24 (2014): 1.
4. Haberstock, "Participatory Description," 133.
5. Haberstock, "Participatory Description," 136.
6. Livia Iacovino, "Shaping and Reshaping Cultural Identity and Memory: Maximising Human Rights through a Participatory Archive," *Archives and Manuscripts* 43, no. 1 (2015): 30.
7. Belinda Battley, "Authenticity in Places of Belonging: Community Collective Memory as a Complex, Adaptive Recordkeeping System," *Archives and Manuscripts* 48, no. 1 (2020): 15.
8. Brian Carpenter, "Archival Initiatives for the Indigenous Collections at the American Philosophical Society," Case 1, Access Policies for Native American Archival Materials—Case Studies (Chicago: Society of American Archivists, 2019), 2, https://www2.archivists.org/sites/all/files/Case_1_Archival_Initiatives_for_Indiginous_Collections.pdf, captured at https://perma.cc/9YQK-NVGR.
9. Carpenter, "Archival Initiatives for the Indigenous Collections," 8–9.
10. Timothy B. Powell, "Digital Knowledge Sharing: Forging Partnerships between Scholars, Archives, and Indigenous Communities," *Museum Anthropology Review* 10, no. 2 (2016): 68.
11. Teodora C. Hasegan, "The Opportunities and Challenges in Managing Indigenous Digital Archives: The Case of the Indigenous Subject Guide at the CNAIR," *Rising Voices*, December 15, 2018, https://rising.globalvoices.org/blog/2018/12/14/the-opportunities-and-challenges-in-managing-indigenous-digital-archives, captured at https://perma.cc/W2KS-QYPY.

12. J. Keri Cronin, "Assimilation and Difference: Two Recent Exhibitions of Archival Photographs," *Archivaria* 54 (2003): 135.
13. *Survivor* is the preferred term for someone who attended residential schools.
14. For more information on this project, see Krista McCracken, "Community Archival Practice: Indigenous Grassroots Collaboration at the Shingwauk Residential Schools Centre," *American Archivist* 78, no. 1 (2015): 181–91, https://doi.org/10.17723/0360-9081.78.1.181.
15. Michelle Caswell, *Archiving the Unspeakable: Silence, Memory and the Photographic Record in Cambodia* (Madison: University of Wisconsin Press, 2014), 96.
16. Aanischaaukamikw Cree Cultural Institute, "Mission and Vision," 2020, https://creeculturalinstitute.ca/about/mission-and-vision.
17. Annie Bosum and Ashley Dunne, "Implementing the Brian Deer Classification Scheme for Aanischaaukamikw Cree Cultural Institute," *Collection Management* 42, no. 3–4 (2017): 282.
18. Gabrielle Gardiner, Jemima McDonald, Alex Byrne, and Kirsten Thorpe, "Respect, Trust and Engagement: Creating an Australian Indigenous Data Archive," *Collection Building* 30, no. 4 (2011): 148–52.
19. Gabrielle Gardiner and Kirsten Thorpe, "The Aboriginal and Torres Strait Islander Data Archive: Connecting Communities and Research Data," *Language Documentation and Description* 12 (2014): 105.
20. Gardiner and Thorpe, "The Aboriginal and Torres Strait Islander Data Archive," 111.
21. Anne J. Gilliland, "Contemplating Co-creator Rights in Archival Description," *Knowledge Organization* 39, no. 5 (2012): 343.
22. Gilliland, "Contemplating Co-creator Rights in Archival Description," 116.
23. Aboriginal and Torres Strait Islander Data Archive, "ATSIDA Protocols," ATSIDA website, https://www.atsida.edu.au/protocols/atsida/principles.
24. Gilliland, "Contemplating Co-creator Rights in Archival Description," 344.
25. For more information on the Trust and Technology Project, which contributed to the development of the KHA, see Shannon Faulkhead, Livia Iacovino, Sue McKemmish, and Kirsten Thorpe, "Australian Indigenous Knowledge and the Archives: Embracing Multiple Ways of Knowing and Keeping," *Archives and Manuscripts* 38, no. 1 (2010): 27–50.
26. Kooramyee Cooper and Sharon Huebner, "Koorie Culture and Technology: A Digital Archive Project for Victorian Koorie Communities," *Archives and Manuscripts* 35, no. 1 (2007): 20.
27. Cooper and Huebner, "Koorie Culture and Technology," 23.
28. Jane Lydon, "Return: The Photographic Archive and Technologies of Indigenous Memory," *Photographies* 3, no. 2 (2010): 179.
29. National Library of New Zealand, "Our History," https://natlib.govt.nz/about-us/our-history.
30. Ariana Tikao and Nicola Frean, "Titiro ki Muri: Surfacing Māori Identity in Archival Collections," Presentation at International Council on Archives, Brisbane, Australia, 2012, 3, http://ica2012.ica.org/files/pdf/Full%20papers%20upload/ica12final00349.pdf, captured at https://perma.cc/FSU8-B9HH.

31. For more information on the relationship of this treaty to archival practice in New Zealand, see chapter two, "Archives and Cultural Protocols."
32. National Library of New Zealand, "Te mauri o te mātauranga: purihia, tiakina! | Principles for the Care and Preservation of Māori Materials," https://natlib.govt.nz/about-us/strategy-and-policy/principles-for-the-care-and-preservation-of-maori-materials.
33. For more information on the treaty and its cultural implications, see David Butts, "Māori, Museums and the Treaty of Waitangi: The Changing Politics of Representation and Control," in *Museum Revolutions: How Museums Change and Are Changed*, edited by Simon Knell, Suzanne MacLeod, and Sheila Watson (New York: Routledge, 2007), 241–53.
34. Butts, "Māori, Museums and the Treaty of Waitangi."
35. Bradford W. Morse, "Indigenous Human Rights and Knowledge in Archives, Museums, and Libraries: Some International Perspectives with Specific Reference to New Zealand and Canada," *Archival Science* 12, no. 2 (2012): 129.
36. Tikao and Frean, "Titiro ki Muri," 3. f.
37. Tikao and Frean, "Titiro ki Muri," 3. f.
38. Daniel Hikuroa, "Mātauranga Māori—The ūkaipō of Knowledge in New Zealand," *Journal of the Royal Society of New Zealand* 47, no. 1 (2017): 5–10.
39. To learn more, visit the Ngā Ūpoko Tukutuk website at https://natlib.govt.nz/librarians/nga-upoko-tukutuku.
40. University of Waikato, "Pei Te Hurinui Jones Papers," O Neherā, https://onehera.waikato.ac.nz/nodes/view/5217.
41. Hēmi Whaanga, David Bainbridge, Michela Anderson, Korii Scrivener, Papitha Cader, Tom Roa, and Te Taka Keegan, "He Matapihi Mā Mua, Mō Muri: The Ethics, Processes, and Procedures Associated with the Digitization of Indigenous Knowledge—The Pei Jones Collection," *Cataloging & Classification Quarterly* 53, no. 5–6 (2015): 520–47.
42. University of Waikato, "Mahi Māreikura," https://www.waikato.ac.nz/library/about/student-centre/taonga/mahi-mareikura.
43. Hemi Whaanga and Rangiiria Hedley, "The Display and Conservation of Taonga Maori-Establishing Culturally Appropriate Display and Conservation Facilities: Mahi Mareikura-a Work in Progress," *He Puna Korero: Journal of Māori and Pacific Development* 7, no. 2 (2006): 12–13.
44. Jessica Tai, "Cultural Humility as a Framework for Anti-Oppressive Archival Description," *Journal of Critical Library and Information Studies* 3, no. 2 (2020): 1–23.
45. There will be cases where it is not the right time for a community project, and while that can interfere with strategic plans or quarterly goals, professionals should keep in mind that appropriate relationships with the proper context are more important than forcing a community to participate in a project to make an organization look good. Furthermore, the authors ask archivists and related professionals to consider the historical context of their institutions and the materials they house. It may be necessary to reexamine the appropriateness of those collections and stories at that institution and if they are that institution's story to tell.

5

Indigenous Archival Futures

ARCHIVISTS, THE ARCHIVES PROFESSION, AND ARCHIVAL ORGANIZA-
tions have work to do. Decentering colonial archival practices will require a lot of active engagement, difficult conversations, meaningful partnerships, and change. The archives profession must prioritize the relationship building the archives profession still needs to do and reimagine how archival practice, research, and community engagement can exist in decolonial frameworks. Archives and archival practice can have imagined futures beyond uses for the colonial state. They can exist beyond the structures created through the legacies of white supremacy and become a part of decolonial power. Likewise, archives can be part of the future of Indigenous communities that are reclaiming and preserving their stories for future generations. This chapter engages in some of this imagining. What might the archival field look like if Indigenous communities controlled more archives? How might archival practice change to further respect Indigenous knowledge? Dana A. Williams and Marissa K. López have argued that:

> If the archive has historically provided an opportunity to establish tradition, the ethnic archive affords an opportunity to the opposite: to challenge assumptions cultivated as truths; to contest the hegemony of the nation-state's imagined pasts and futures; and to invoke a multiethnic cacophony of voices that require reconsiderations of established knowledge and knowledge production alike.[1]

Indigenous archives and the use of archives by Indigenous communities can change the way that archives function, expose new narratives told by archival records, and establish new ways of knowing the past. Evelyn Wareham has described settler-colonial archives "[l]ike the glass cases of museums, the archives of colonial regimes and their independent successor states have often been described as prisons for the identities of the oppressed."[2] For Indigenous communities accessing archives, there is potential for archives to become sites of reclamation for at-risk knowledges. But this is only possible when barriers are broken down and Indigenous peoples are given control of how archival materials are shared, cared for, and maintained. Indigenous advocates in the United States and Australia have proclaimed that their people are "captives" of archives; their pasts are caught in records created by others, to which archivists hold the keys.[3] Advocacy organizations such as the Association of Tribal Archives, Libraries, and Museums (ATALM) are pushing back against mainstream archival practice and supporting Indigenous-run community archives in the United States. ATALM represents tribal museums, archives, libraries, and allied individuals who strongly advocate for the rights of Indigenous nations to maintain their own archives and heritage organizations.[4] ATALM is one example of an advocacy organization creating and supporting spaces for Indigenous archival sovereignty and Indigenous-driven archival futures understood in Indigenous terms.

Camille Callison describes archives, alongside libraries and museums, from a Tāłtān Nation perspective, as a "new canoe" that can be used to "carry on language and culture to future generations."[5] Archives can be integral parts of Indigenous community history, narratives, and futures. They can preserve important cultural information and continue to share that information with future generations. Archives can also be part of reclaiming culture, language, and traditions within Indigenous communities. The sites can be cultural hubs or community spaces that bring the historical into the present through direct links to knowledge from the past or accounts from community Elders. This can only be the case if Indigenous knowledges and ways of doing are embedded within archives and if archives are open to working with Indigenous communities. This structure cannot be superficial or half-hearted. Archives need to have integrity to honor the wishes of community members. As Crystal Fraser and Zoe Todd have asserted, "To reclaim, reshape, and transform the archives to meet the needs of Indigenous peoples requires an honest and blunt engagement with the bureaucratic and arcane structures that govern and shape research today."[6] It is necessary to critically examine and acknowledge the colonial roots of archives and be honest about what changes are possible within archival practice. Community-driven, Indigenous-led archives can potentially address the need to decolonize history and research. Further, rethinking archival practice is important to understand the past and imagine the future of Indigenous communities. Indeed, connections between archival reimaging can be made to future studies and the concept of Indigenous futurism. Indigenous futurism "creates room for Indigenous culture to reclaim their place in the present."[7] Indigenous futurism importantly acknowledges the complexity of Indigenous peoples as nonstatic people of the present and part of the future— not just part of the past. Indigenous futurism also moves beyond colonialism and victimization narratives to start seeing Indigenous life through the lens of culture and Indigenous ways of knowing. The future of archives—specifically decolonized and community-driven archives—needs to include Indigenous peoples and their worldviews. Speaking of education and colonization, Leanne Betasamosake Simpson has argued that "[t]he academic industrial complex does not and cannot provide the proper context for Nishnaabeg intelligence without the full, valued recognition of the context within which Nishnaabeg intelligence manifests itself – the *practice* of aki – freedom, sovereignty and self-determination over bodies, minds and land."[8] We argue the same is true for archival practice. Archival practice cannot be decolonized without recognizing Indigenous sovereignty over land, ideas, and culture. This sovereignty needs to be embedded into the ways archives organize material, how archival practice is taught in postsecondary education, and how archivists work with Indigenous communities. Further, archival practice needs to make space for Indigenous peoples to have gainful employment in archives, placing them in leadership positions that can give them the capacity to do essential systems change work. Without Indigenous peoples at the forefront, Indigenous sovereignty cannot be embedded into archival systems.

From my perspective (Skylee-Storm) and lived experience as an Indigenous person working in archives and as a researcher, I see decolonial archival futures as a necessary step to decolonizing academic scholarship and education at all levels. Because archives inform our understanding and organization of the past, I imagine our archival futures as supporting, affirming, and acknowledging Indigenous nations' unique existences and sovereignty. This future includes policies that make provisions for nations that wish to repatriate items to their own archives and for established archives to support Indigenous nations in establishing a functioning archive that serves their community. While digitization and digital repatriation initiatives are significant, many communities in Canada cannot access those solutions due to the lack of high-speed Internet access. Further, archives set up for the community by the community have more meaning and usefulness, even when the records come from government sources. While these imagined futures are all subject to the lack of financing and resources that archives face, there are ways archives can start transforming their archival practice through policy and relationships.

Areas for Transformation of Archival Practice

The final section of this chapter focuses on areas where archives and archival practice can be changed to better align with the needs of diverse Indigenous communities. Each Indigenous community has its own needs and priorities, and there is no one-size-fits-all solution to the colonial nature of archives. Archives should work with Indigenous communities to determine how best to change their practices to best serve the needs of Indigenous peoples who have ties to their holdings. These changes are going to take time, effort, and commitment. This is important work that can dramatically impact the experience of Indigenous peoples who access archival spaces and services.

1. Root archival practice in the United Nations Declaration on the Rights of Indigenous Peoples. Recognize the inherent right of Indigenous self-determination and the right of Indigenous peoples to control records by and about them.[9] Prioritizing the needs and rights of Indigenous peoples to control their own records means involving Indigenous peoples in every part of the archival process—from acquisition to description to access. This should be for records already held by archives as well as records that archives are looking to acquire if they relate to Indigenous peoples. Respect Indigenous sovereignty through all forms of archival practice.
2. Include decolonial archival frameworks in archival education. New professionals should learn about Indigenous communities and Indigenous archival practices as part of archival studies. This education work also needs to be included in professional development opportunities, as many senior archivists still have a lot to learn about decolonial approaches to archival practice, which includes understanding regionally relevant frameworks that can guide policy and practices toward Indigenous sovereignty. Archives professionals should keep in mind that building relationships that make space for Indigenous community members to lead in proper cultural care for collections is vital in establishing a relationship built on Indigenous sovereignty.
3. Situate archival work in respectful relationships and recognize that relationship building is an ongoing process that takes time and

effort. Decolonial archival practice cannot happen in isolation, rather it needs to occur in the context of community.
4. Decolonial archival work should be intergenerational. This means engaging Elders, youth, and people of all ages in archival practice. Engagement can occur through conversations about archival records, sharing materials in the community, or advisory groups who oversee decolonial archival approaches.
5. Respect ceremony and cultural protocols. Indigenous communities will know when ceremony is needed and what cultural protocols are necessary for a particular archives or set of archival materials. Archival organizations and archivists need to listen and respect ceremonies. This might mean creating spaces where smudging and other ceremonies can happen within an archival building. It might also mean returning materials to the community for them to be put to rest through ceremonies. It is important to note that not all items are meant to live forever, which runs counter to Western policies of conservation.
6. Recognize the Indigenous right of reply, which "is the ability to challenge the depiction of individuals, objects or events presented in records by providing a self-determined response to both the record itself and the metadata associated with it."[10] The right of reply can change the historical narrative and provide an Indigenous-led interpretation of the past. This allows for the insertion of Indigenous knowledge and Indigenous worldviews into the archival record, alongside colonial documents and colonial viewpoints.
7. Community engagement and participatory archival practices are key to transforming archival practice from a one-sided information-seeking relationship to one that actively supports the needs of Indigenous peoples. Participatory archives recognize the value of collaboration and building reciprocal, respectful relationships. Participatory archival practice can take many shapes: redescription projects, the development of Indigenous-centered taxonomies, the prioritization of Indigenous ownership rights, and more. Participatory archives should not be an additional burden on Indigenous peoples, rather they should be based on reciprocity and the needs of Indigenous peoples.
8. Acknowledge that multiple forms of provenance and ownership exist. Records can have multiple creators, including entire Indigenous communities. Western forms of copyright do not adequately encompass Indigenous intellectual property rights, and archives

need to acknowledge the problematic nature of basing decisions for Indigenous materials on Western concepts such as copyright.
9. The physical spaces of archives need to be more accommodating to the needs of Indigenous communities. This means reexamining ID requirements, security processes, and the physical organization of spaces. Aspects of physical spaces that should be considered include, but are not limited to, physical seating, wall colors, and sounds within a space. Archives, particularly those that are extensions of government or other public and private institutions, can be physically stressful, hostile, and unwelcoming to Indigenous researchers. This is especially true for archival spaces where security cameras or armed guards are present because this replicates the colonial policing and justice systems that persecute and threaten Indigenous communities daily. This needs to change.[11]
10. In order to move forward, it is imperative that archives professionals recognize that colonial archives are inherently problematic and tell only one side of the historical narrative. Colonial archives are extractive archives, having decontextualized Indigenous knowledge, history, and information. Records from colonial archives need to be reconnected with the Indigenous communities they are written by and about, allowing for the reshaping of the historical record.

These recommendations are just that, recommendations. They are not prescriptive, definitive, or the only way to approach decolonial archival practice. Respectful relationships, Indigenous sovereignty, ongoing conversations, and the willingness to let Indigenous communities take the lead need to be at the center of decolonizing archival practices. Imagining the possibilities of archives led by Indigenous communities is an important part of situating archives in not only the present but also the future of Indigenous communities. This book is a reflection and a learning journey of the authors' experiences in the archives profession and, on the other side, as research historians. Their working knowledge comes from a place of Indigenous community-based archival practice. The authors invite readers to continue pushing the boundaries of archival practice, building relationships, and challenging colonial ways of organizing information. Although it can be difficult to effect change within institutional hierarchies, it is imperative to make small changes and let relationships influence and guide the way to real systems change. Through imagining and pushing back, new ways of engaging with archives can take hold and transform archival practice.

NOTES

1. Dana A. Williams and Marissa K. Lopez, "More Than a Fever: Toward a Theory of the Ethnic Archive," *PMLA/Publications of the Modern Language Association of America* 127, no. 2 (2012): 358.
2. Evelyn Wareham, "'Our Own Identity, Our Own Taonga, Our Own Self Coming Back': Indigenous Voices in New Zealand Record-Keeping," *Archivaria* 52 (2001): 27.
3. Wareham, "'Our Own Identity,'" 27.
4. Holly Witchey, "Tribal Archives, Libraries and Museums: ATALM, A Practical Model for Local Collaboration," in *Economic Considerations for Libraries, Archives and Museums*, edited by Lorraine A. Stuart, Thomas F. R. Clareson, and Joyce Ray (New York: Routledge, 2022), 77–88.
5. Camille Callison, "Indigenous Peoples' New Canoe," in *Aboriginal and Visible Minority Librarians: Oral Histories from Canada*, edited by Deborah Lee and Mahalakshmi Kumaran (Washington, DC: Rowman & Littlefield, 2014): 135.
6. Crystal Fraser and Zoe Todd, "Decolonial Sensibilities: Indigenous Research and Engaging with Archives in Contemporary Colonial Canada," *L'internationale* (2016), https://www.internationaleonline.org/research/decolonising_practices/54_decolonial_sensibilities_indigenous_research_and_engaging_with_archives_in_contemporary_colonial_canada, captured at https://perma.cc/LAL6-RJJJ.
7. Samantha Matters, "Strategic Foresight in Métis Communities: Lessons from Indigenous Futurism," (master's thesis, Ontario College of Art and Design University, 2019): 7, http://openresearch.ocadu.ca/id/eprint/2804/1/Matters_Samantha_2019_MDES_SFI_MRP.pdf, captured at https://perma.cc/QF4Q-BTDV.
8. Leanne Betasamosake Simpson, "Land as Pedagogy: Nishnaabeg Intelligence and Rebellious Transformation," *Decolonization: Indigeneity, Education & Society* 3, no. 3 (2014): 17. Emphasis in original.
9. United Nations, "United Nations Declaration on the Rights of Indigenous Peoples," https://www.un.org/development/desa/indigenouspeoples/declaration-on-the-rights-of-indigenous-peoples.html.
10. Indigenous Archives Collective, "Indigenous Archives Collective Position Statement on the Right of Reply to Indigenous Knowledges and Information Held in Archives," https://indigenousarchives.net/indigenous-archives-collective-position-statement-on-the-right-of-reply-to-indigenous-knowledges-and-information-held-in-archives.
11. For more information on the physical spaces of archives and the needs of Indigenous researchers, see Krista McCracken and Skylee-Storm Hogan, "Laughter Filled the Space," *The International Journal of Information, Diversity, & Inclusion* 5, no. 1 (2021): 97–110.

Bibliography

Aanischaaukamikw Cree Cultural Institute. "Mission and Vision." 2020. https://creeculturalinstitute.ca/about/mission-and-vision.

Aboriginal and Torres Strait Islander Data Archive. "ATSIDA Protocols." ATSIDA website. Accessed December 5, 2022. https://www.atsida.edu.au/protocols/atsida/principles.

Aboriginal and Torres Strait Islander Library, Information and Resource Network Inc. "Governance and Management." 2012. https://atsilirn.aiatsis.gov.au/protocols.php.

———. "Intellectual Property." 2012. https://atsilirn.aiatsis.gov.au/protocols.php.

———. "The Protocols Are . . ." 2012. https://atsilirn.aiatsis.gov.au/protocols.php.

———. "The Protocols Are Not . . ." 2012. https://atsilirn.aiatsis.gov.au/protocols.php.

Albritton, Thomas P. "The Myth of the Vanishing Race: Interpreting Historical Photographs of Native Americans." Master's thesis, Boise State University, 2021.

American Philosophical Society. "The American Philosophical Society *Protocols for the Treatment of Indigenous Materials*." 2017. https://www.amphilsoc.org/sites/default/files/2017-11/attachments/APS%20Protocols.pdf, captured at https://perma.cc/ZS7Y-87DM.

Anderson, Jane, and Greg Younging. "Renegotiated Relationships and New Understandings: Indigenous Protocols." In *Free Knowledge: Confronting the*

Commodification of Human Discovery, edited by Patricia Elliot and Daryl Hepting, 180–98. University of Regina Press, 2015.

Association of Canadian Archivists. "Reconciliation Framework: The Response to the Report of the Truth and Reconciliation Commission Taskforce." *Archivists.ca*. March 22, 2022. https://www.archivists.ca/Latest-News-Announcements/12676249.

Australian Human Rights Commission. "UN Declaration on the Rights of Indigenous Peoples." Accessed December 6, 2022. https://humanrights.gov.au/our-work/aboriginal-and-torres-strait-islander-social-justice/projects/un-declaration-rights.

Bak, Greg. "An Archival Overview of the TRC's Calls to Action." *Fonds d'Archives* 1 (2017): 1–21. https://fondsdarchives.ca/index.php/fondsdarchives/article/view/3/2.

Barker, Adam J. *Settler: Identity and Colonialism in 21st Century Canada*. Halifax: Fernwood Publishing Co. Ltd., 2015.

Bastian, Jeannette Allis. "Reading Colonial Records through an Archival Lens: The Provenance of Place, Space and Creation." *Archival Science* 6, no. 3–4 (2006): 267–84.

Battley, Belinda. "Authenticity in Places of Belonging: Community Collective Memory as a Complex, Adaptive Recordkeeping System." *Archives and Manuscripts* 48, no. 1 (2020): 59–79.

Beebe, Laura L. "Unsettling the Archive: Dis-imagining Colonial Subjects to Re-imagine Knowledge Production." Dissertation, University of California, San Diego, 2012.

Boles, Frank, David George-Shongo, and Christine Weideman. *Report: Task Force to Review Protocols for Native American Archival Materials*. Chicago: Society of American Archivists, 2008, 3–20. http://files.archivists.org/governance/taskforces/0208-NativeAmProtocols-IIIA.pdf, captured at https://perma.cc/ACJ5-CK6Q.

Bosum, Annie, and Ashley Dunne. "Implementing the Brian Deer Classification Scheme for Aanischaaukamikw Cree Cultural Institute." *Collection Management* 42, no. 3–4 (2017): 280–93.

The British Crown. "The Treaty of Waitangi, 1840." https://nzhistory.govt.nz/files/documents/treaty-kawharu-footnotes.pdf.

Buchanan, Rachel. "Decolonizing the Archives: The Work of New Zealand's Waitangi Tribunal." *Public History Review* 14 (2007): 44–63. https://doi.org/10.5130/phrj.v14i0.399.

Butts, David. "Māori, Museums and the Treaty of Waitangi: The Changing Politics of Representation and Control." In *Museum Revolutions: How*

Museums Change and Are Changed, edited by Simon Knell, Suzanne MacLeod, and Sheila Watson, 241–53. New York: Routledge, 2007.

Callison, Camille. "Indigenous Peoples' New Canoe." In *Aboriginal and Visible Minority Librarians: Oral Histories from Canada*, edited by Deborah Lee and Mahalakshmi Kumaran, 135–46. Washington, DC: Rowman & Littlefield Publishers, 2014.

Carlisle Indian School Digital Resource Centre. "About." Accessed December 5, 2022. https://carlisleindian.dickinson.edu/page/about.

———. "Student Records." Accessed December 5, 2022. https://carlisleindian.dickinson.edu/student_records.

Carpenter, Brian. "Archival Initiatives for the Indigenous Collections at the American Philosophical Society." Case 1, Access Policies for Native American Archival Materials—Case Studies. Chicago, Society of American Archivists, 2019. https://www2.archivists.org/sites/all/files/Case_1_Archival_Initiatives_for_Indiginous_Collections.pdf, captured at https://perma.cc/9YQK-NVGR.

Caswell, Michelle. *Archiving the Unspeakable: Silence, Memory and the Photographic Record in Cambodia*. Madison: University of Wisconsin Press, 2014.

Christen, Kimberly. "Archival Challenges and Digital Solutions in Aboriginal Australia." *SAA Archaeological Recorder* 8, no. 2 (2008): 21–24.

———. "Gone Digital: Aboriginal Remix and the Cultural Commons." *International Journal of Cultural Property* 12 (2005): 315–45.

———. "Opening Archives: Respectful Repatriation." *American Archivist* 74, no. 1 (2011): 185–210. https://doi.org/10.17723/aarc.74.1.4233nv6nv6428521.

———, Alex Merrill, and Michael Wynne. "A Community of Relations: Mukurtu Hubs and Spokes." *D-Lib Magazine* 23, no. 5/6 (2017).

Commission on Human Rights Submission of Discrimination and Protection of Minorities Working Group on Indigenous Peoples. *The Mataatua Declaration on Cultural and Intellectual Property Rights of Indigenous Peoples*. July 1993. https://www.wipo.int/export/sites/www/tk/en/databases/creative_heritage/docs/mataatua.pdf, captured at https://perma.cc/6HQA-R48S.

Cook, Terry. "'We Are What We Keep; We Keep What We Are': Archival Appraisal Past, Present and Future." *Journal of the Society of Archivists* 32, no. 2 (2011): 173–89.

Cooper, Kooramyee, and Sharon Huebner. "Koorie Culture and Technology: A Digital Archive Project for Victorian Koorie Communities." *Archives and Manuscripts* 35, no. 1 (2007): 18–32.

Cox, Richard J. "American Archival History: Its Development, Needs, and Opportunities." *American Archivist* 46, no. 1 (1983): 31–41. https://doi.org/10.17723/aarc.46.1.n43kl32721m250g1.

Cronin, J. Keri. "Assimilation and Difference: Two Recent Exhibitions of Archival Photographs." *Archivaria* 54 (Fall 2003): 130–41.

Croswell, Debra. "As Days Go By: An Introduction." In *Wiyaxayxt / Wiyaakaa'awn / As Days Go By Our History, Our Land, Our People*, edited by Jennifer Karson. Seattle: University of Washington Press, 2014.

Douglas, Jennifer. "Origins and Beyond: The Ongoing Evolution of Archival Ideas about Provenance." In *Currents of Archival Thinking*, edited by Heather MacNeil and Terry Eastwood, 2nd ed. Santa Barbara, CA: Libraries Unlimited, 2017.

Duranti, Luciana. "The Archival Body of Knowledge: Archival Theory, Method, and Practice, and Graduate and Continuing Education." *Journal of Education for Library and Information Science* 34, no. 1 (1993): 8–24. https://doi.org/10.2307/40323707.

Faulkhead, Shannon, Livia Iacovino, Sue McKemmish, and Kirsten Thorpe. "Australian Indigenous Knowledge and the Archives: Embracing Multiple Ways of Knowing and Keeping." *Archives and Manuscripts* 38, no. 1 (2010): 27–50.

First Nations Circle. "Home." 2007. https://www2.nau.edu/libnap-p.

———. "Protocols for Native American Archival Materials." 2007. https://www2.nau.edu/libnap-p/protocols.html, captured at https://perma.cc/PUE2-F9ND.

Fraser, Crystal, and Zoe Todd. "Decolonial Sensibilities: Indigenous Research and Engaging with Archives in Contemporary Colonial Canada." *L'internationale* (2016). https://www.internationaleonline.org/research/decolonising_practices/54_decolonial_sensibilities_indigenous_research_and_engaging_with_archives_in_contemporary_colonial_canada, captured at https://perma.cc/LAL6-RJJJ.

Free, David. "ACRL Endorses Protocols for Native American Materials." *ACRL Insider*. February 5, 2020. https://acrl.ala.org/acrlinsider/archives/19019.

Gardiner, Gabrielle, and Kirsten Thorpe. "The Aboriginal and Torres Strait Islander Data Archive: Connecting Communities and Research Data." *Language Documentation and Description* 12 (2014): 103–19.

Gardiner, Gabrielle, Jemima McDonald, Alex Byrne, and Kirsten Thorpe. "Respect, Trust and Engagement: Creating an Australian Indigenous Data Archive." *Collection Building* 30, no. 4 (2011): 148–52.

Garwood-Houng, Alana, and Fiona Blackburn. "The ATSILIRN Protocols: A Twenty-First Century Guide to Appropriate Library Services for and about

Aboriginal and Torres Strait Islander Peoples." *The Australian Library Journal* 63, no. 1 (2014): 4–15.

———. "Tracking the ATSILIRN Protocols: Maintaining the Focus on Indigenous Library Issues." Presentation at the Australian Library and Information Association Biennial Conference, Alice Springs, Australia, September 5, 2008.

Ghaddar, J. J. "The Spectre in the Archive: Truth, Reconciliation, and Indigenous Archival Memory." *Archivaria* 82, no. 1 (2016): 3–26.

———, and Michelle Caswell. "'To Go Beyond': Towards a Decolonial Archival Praxis." *Archival Science* 19, no. 2 (2019): 71–85.

Gilliland, Anne J. "Contemplating Co-creator Rights in Archival Description." *Knowledge Organization* 39, no. 5 (2012): 340–46.

———, and Sue McKemmish. "The Role of Participatory Archives in Furthering Human Rights, Reconciliation and Recovery." *Atlanti: Review for Modern Archival Theory and Practice* 24 (2014): 78–88.

Government of Canada. "Implementing the United Nations Declaration on the Rights of Indigenous Peoples in Canada." *Government of Canada.* 2021. https://www.justice.gc.ca/eng/declaration/index.html.

Government of New Zealand. "Public Records Act." 2005. https://legislation.govt.nz/act/public/2005/0040/latest/DLM345529.html.

Haberstock, Lauren. "Participatory Description: Decolonizing Descriptive Methodologies in Archives." *Archival Science* 20, no. 2 (2020): 125–38.

Hall, Claire. "Mukurtu for Mātauranga Māori: A Case Study in Indigenous Archiving for Reo and Tikanga Revitalisation." *Language, Culture & Technology* (2017): 193.

Harkin, Natalie. "The Poetics of (Re)Mapping Archives: Memory in the Blood." *Journal of the Association for the Study of Australian Literature* 14, no. 3 (2014): 1–14.

Hasegan, Teodora C. "The Opportunities and Challenges in Managing Indigenous Digital Archives: The Case of the Indigenous Subject Guide at the CNAIR." *Rising Voices*, December 15, 2018. https://rising.globalvoices.org/blog/2018/12/14/the-opportunities-and-challenges-in-managing-indigenous-digital-archives, captured at https://perma.cc/W2KS-QYPY.

Hernandez-Read, Erica. "SCCA – Response to the Report of the Truth and Reconciliation Commission Task Force (TRC-TF), Appendix E: Action Plan (v. 6)," Steering Committee on Canada's Archives. April 5, 2017. https://archives2026.files.wordpress.com/2017/05/2c-en-trc-action-plan-v-6_5-april-2017.pdf, captured at https://perma.cc/Z5JQ-VPN9.

Hikuroa, Daniel. "Mātauranga Māori—The ūkaipō of Knowledge in New Zealand." *Journal of the Royal Society of New Zealand* 47, no. 1 (2017): 5–10.

Hunt, Dallas. "Nikîkîwân 1: Contesting Settler Colonial Archives through Indigenous Oral History." *Canadian Literature* 230/231 (2016): 25–42.

Iacovino, Livia. "Rethinking Archival, Ethical and Legal Frameworks for Records of Indigenous Australian Communities: A Participant Relationship Model of Rights and Responsibilities." *Archival Science* 10, no. 4 (2010): 353–72.

———. "Shaping and Reshaping Cultural Identity and Memory: Maximising Human Rights through a Participatory Archive." *Archives and Manuscripts* 43, no. 1 (2015): 29–41.

Indigenous Archives Collective. "Indigenous Archives Collective Position Statement on the Right of Reply to Indigenous Knowledges and Information Held in Archives." https://indigenousarchives.net/indigenous-archives-collective-position-statement-on-the-right-of-reply-to-indigenous-knowledges-and-information-held-in-archives.

Indigenous and Northern Affairs Canada. "Canada's Statement of Support on the United Nations Declaration on the Rights of Indigenous Peoples." November 12, 2010. https://www.aadnc-aandc.gc.ca/eng/1309374239861/1309374546142.

Irlbacher-Fox, Stephanie. "Traditional Knowledge, Co-existence and Co-resistance." *Decolonization: Indigeneity, Education & Society* 3, no. 3 (2014): 145–58.

Irons Walch, Victoria. "Introduction." In *Standards for Archival Description: A Handbook*. Chicago: Society of American Archivists, 1994. http://www.archivists.org/catalog/stds99/intro.html, captured at https://perma.cc/Y3CM-KWX8.

Joffrion, Elizabeth, and Natalia Fernández. "Collaborations between Tribal and Nontribal Organizations: Suggested Best Practices for Sharing Expertise, Cultural Resources, and Knowledge." *American Archivist* 78, no. 1 (2015): 192–237. https://doi.org/10.17723/0360-9081.78.1.192.

Ka'ai-Mahuta, Rachael. "The Use of Digital Technology in the Preservation of Māori Song." *Te Kaharoa* 5, no. 1 (2012): 99–108.

Karuk Tribe. "About." *Sípnuuk*. 2014. https://sipnuuk.karuk.us/about.

———. "Browse Collections." *Sípnuuk*. Accessed December 5, 2022. https://sipnuuk.karuk.us/collections.

———, Lisa Hillman, Leaf Hillman, Adrienne R. S. Harling, Bari Talley, and Angela McLaughlin. "Building Sípnuuk: A Digital Library, Archives, and Museum for Indigenous Peoples." *Collection Management* 42, no. 3–4 (2017): 394–16. https://doi.org/10.1080/01462679.2017.1331870.

Kelleher, Christian. "Archives Without Archives: (Re)Locating and (Re)Defining the Archive through Post-Custodial Praxis." *Journal of Critical Library and Information Studies* 1, no. 2 (2017): 1–30.

Leslie, John F. "The Indian Act: An Historical Perspective." *Canadian Parliamentary Review* 25, no. 2 (2002): 23–27.

Lorde, Audre. *Sister Outsider: Essays and Speeches*. Crossing Press, 2007.

Lowman, Emma Battell, and Adam J. Barker. *Settler: Identity and Colonialism in 21st Century Canada*. Halifax: Fernwood Publishing Co. Ltd., 2015.

Lydon, Jane. "Return: The Photographic Archive and Technologies of Indigenous Memory." *Photographies* 3, no. 2 (2010): 173–87.

Matters, Samantha. "Strategic Foresight in Métis Communities: Lessons from Indigenous Futurism." Master's thesis, Ontario College of Art and Design University, 2019. http://openresearch.ocadu.ca/id/eprint/2804/1/Matters_Samantha_2019_MDES_SFI_MRP.pdf, captured at https://perma.cc/QF4Q-BTDV.

McCracken, Krista. "Community Archival Practice: Indigenous Grassroots Collaboration at the Shingwauk Residential Schools Centre." *American Archivist* 78, no. 1 (2015): 181–91. https://doi.org/10.17723/0360-9081.78.1.181.

———, and Skylee-Storm Hogan. "Laughter Filled the Space." *The International Journal of Information, Diversity, & Inclusion* 5, no. 1 (2021): 97–110.

McKemmish, Sue, Shannon Faulkhead, and Lynette Russell. "Distrust in the Archive: Reconciling Records." *Archival Science* 11, no. 3–4 (2011): 211–39.

Millar, Laura. "The Death of the Fonds and the Resurrection of Provenance: Archival Context in Space and Time." *Archivaria* (2002): 1–15.

Ministry of Māori Development. "UN Declaration on the Rights of Indigenous Peoples." https://www.tpk.govt.nz/en/whakamahia/un-declaration-on-the-rights-of-indigenous-peoples.

Moen, Kelsey. "Moving Forward: Shifting Perspectives on the 'Protocols for Native American Archival Materials' in the Archives Community." Master's thesis, University of North Carolina at Chapel Hill, 2018. https://doi.org/10.17615/4kn3-y652.

Morse, Bradford W. "Indigenous Human Rights and Knowledge in Archives, Museums, and Libraries: Some International Perspectives with Specific Reference to New Zealand and Canada." *Archival Science* 12, no. 2 (2012): 113–40.

Mukurtu. "About Mukurtu." 2020. https://mukurtu.org/about.

———. "Getting Started with Mukurtu CMS." 2020. https://mukurtu.org/support/getting-started-with-mukurtu-cms.

———. "Mukurtu Wumpurrarni-Kari Archive." 2020. https://mukurtu.org/project/mukurtu-wumpurrarni-kari-archive/.

———. "What Is Mukurtu?" 2020. https://mukurtu.org/support/what-is-mukurtu.

Nagle, Peter, and Richard Summerrell. *Aboriginal Deaths in Custody: The Royal Commission and Its Records, 1987–91* (Canberra, A.C.T.: Australian Archives, 2002).

National Archives and Records Administration. "About the National Archives of the United States." *National Archives and Records Administration.* https://www.archives.gov/publications/general-info-leaflets/1-about-archives.html.

———. "American Indian Records in the National Archives." *National Archives and Records Administration.* https://www.archives.gov/research/native-americans.

———. "Researching an Individual or Family." *National Archives and Records Administration.* https://www.archives.gov/research/native-americans/research-individual.

National Archives of Australia. "Bringing Them Home Name Index." https://www.naa.gov.au/explore-collection/first-australians/bringing-them-home-name-index.

———. "Our History." https://www.naa.gov.au/about-us/our-organisation/our-history.

National Library of New Zealand. "Te mauri o te mātauranga: purihia, tiakina! | Principles for the Care and Preservation of Māori Materials." https://natlib.govt.nz/about-us/strategy-and-policy/principles-for-the-care-and-preservation-of-maori-materials.

———. "Our History." https://natlib.govt.nz/about-us/our-history.

Nesmith, Tom. "The Concept of Societal Provenance and Records of Nineteenth-Century Aboriginal–European Relations in Western Canada: Implications for Archival Theory and Practice." *Archival Science* 6, no. 3–4 (2006): 351–60.

Ngā Ūpoko Tukutuk. "Ngā Ūpoko Tukutuk." 2022. https://natlib.govt.nz/librarians/nga-upoko-tukutuku.

Povinelli, Elizabeth A. "The Woman on the Other Side of the Wall: Archiving the Otherwise in Postcolonial Digital Archives." *differences* 22, no. 1 (2011): 146–71.

Powell, Timothy B. "Digital Knowledge Sharing: Forging Partnerships between Scholars, Archives, and Indigenous Communities." *Museum Anthropology Review* 10, no. 2 (2016): 66–90.

Pringle, Jonathan. "Northern Arizona University's Cline Library and the *Protocols*." Case 2, Access Policies for Native American Archival Materials—Case Studies. Chicago: Society of American Archivists, 2019. https://www2.archivists.org/sites/all/files/Case_2_NAU_Cline_Library_and_Protocols.pdf, captured at https://perma.cc/38TV-DLPG.

Response to the Report of the Truth and Reconciliation Commission Taskforce of the Steering Committee on Canada's Archives. *A Reconciliation Framework for Canadian Archives Draft for Public Review*, 2020. https://archives2026.files.wordpress.com/2020/07/reconciliationframework forarchives_july2020_en.pdf.

Rowe, Aimee Carrillo, and Eve Tuck. "Settler Colonialism and Cultural Studies: Ongoing Settlement, Cultural Production, and Resistance." *Cultural Studies ↔ Critical Methodologies* 17, no. 1 (2017): 3–13.

Royal Commission on Aboriginal Peoples. *Report of the Royal Commission on Aboriginal Peoples*, vol. 5: Renewal: A Twenty-Year Commitment. Ottawa: Minister of Supply and Services Canada, 1996.

Schwartz, Joan M., and Terry Cook. "Archives, Records, and Power: The Making of Modern Memory." *Archival Science* 2, no. 1 (2002): 1–19.

Sinclair, Niigaanwewidam James, and Sharon Dainard. "Sixties Scoop." *The Canadian Encyclopedia*. Historica Canada. Article published June 21, 2016. Last edited November 13, 2020. https://www.thecanadianencyclopedia.ca/en/article/sixties-scoop.

Simpson, Leanne Betasamosake. "Land as Pedagogy: Nishnaabeg Intelligence and Rebellious Transformation." *Decolonization: Indigeneity, Education & Society* 3, no. 3 (2014): 1–25.

Smith, Peter. "US Report Details Church-State Collusion on Native Schools." Associated Press, May 14, 2022. https://apnews.com/article/canada-religion-education-native-americans-cultures-87a09745351c02236b99e2955785e1f7, captured at https://perma.cc/K8AM-38B3.

Society of American Archivists. "Access Policies for Native American Archival Materials—Case Studies." https://www2.archivists.org/publications/epubs/Native-American-Archival-Materials-Case-Studies.

———. "Protocols for Native American Archival Materials: Information and Resources Page." 2023. https://www2.archivists.org/groups/native-american-archives-section/protocols-for-native-american-archival-materials-information-and-resources-page.

———. "SAA Council Endorsement of Protocols of Native American Archival Materials." September 14, 2018. https://www2.archivists.org/statements/saa-council-endorsement-of-protocols-for-native-american-archival-materials, captured at https://perma.cc/J73S-W86R.

Steering Committee on Canada's Archives. "About Us." 2023. https://archives2026.com/about.

Tai, Jessica. "Cultural Humility as a Framework for Anti-Oppressive Archival Description." *Journal of Critical Library and Information Studies* 3, no. 2 (2020): 1–23.

Taiaiake Alfred, Gerald. "Colonialism and State Dependency." *Journal of Aboriginal Health* 42 (November 2009): 48, https://jps.library.utoronto.ca/index.php/ijih/article/view/28982/23931.

Tāmata Toiere. "About This Site." *Tāmata Toiere.* 2023. http://www.waiata.maori.nz/en/about.

Te Reo o Taranaki. "Te Pūtē Routiriata o Taranaki Archive." 2022. https://tereootaranaki.org/te-pute-routiriata/.

Thorpe, Kirsten. "Transformative Praxis-Building Spaces for Indigenous Self-Determination in Libraries and Archives." *In the Library with the Lead Pipe.* 2019. https://www.inthelibrarywiththeleadpipe.org/2019/transformative-praxis.

Tikao, Ariana, and Nicola Frean. "Titiro ki Muri: Surfacing Māori Identity in Archival Collections." Presentation at International Council on Archives, Brisbane, Australia, 2012. http://ica2012.ica.org/files/pdf/Full%20papers%20upload/ica12final00349.pdf, captured at https://perma.cc/FSU8-B9HH.

Trouillot, Michel-Rolph. *Silencing the Past: Power and the Production of History.* Boston: Beacon Press, 2015.

Truth and Reconciliation Commission of Canada. *Canada's Residential Schools: The History, Part 1, Origins to 1939: The Final Report of the Truth and Reconciliation Commission of Canada,* vol. 1. Montreal and Kingston: McGill-Queen's University Press, 2015.

———. *Canada's Residential Schools: Reconciliation: The Final Report of the Truth and Reconciliation Commission of Canada,* vol. 6. Montreal and Kingston: McGill-Queen's University Press, 2015.

———. "Calls to Action." 2015. https://ehprnh2mwo3.exactdn.com/wp-content/uploads/2021/01/Calls_to_Action_English2.pdf, captured at https://perma.cc/2KQC-AFDV.

———. *What We Have Learned: Principles of Truth and Reconciliation,* 2015. https://ehprnh2mwo3.exactdn.com/wp-content/uploads/2021/01/Principles_English_Web.pdf, captured at https://perma.cc/C22B-ECY7.

Tuck, Eve, and K. Wayne Yang. "Decolonization Is Not a Metaphor." *Decolonization: Indigeneity, Education & Society* 1, no. 1 (2012): 1–40.

Tuhiwai Smith, Linda. *Decolonizing Methodologies: Research and Indigenous Peoples.* Otago, London, and New York: Zed Books and Otago University Press, 1999.

Underhill, Karen J. "Protocols for Native American Archival Materials." *RBM: A Journal of Rare Books, Manuscripts, and Cultural Heritage* 7, no. 2 (2006): 134–45.

United Nations. Article 12. *Declaration on the Rights of Indigenous Peoples,* 2007. www.un.org/esa/socdev/unpfii/documents/DRIPS_en.pdf, captured at https://perma.cc/HRV8-4R36.

———. Article 29. *Declaration on the Rights of Indigenous Peoples,* 2007. www.un.org/esa/socdev/unpfii/documents/DRIPS_en.pdf, captured at https://perma.cc/HRV8-4R36.

———. Article 31, *Declaration on the Rights of Indigenous Peoples,* 2007. www.un.org/esa/socdev/unpfii/documents/DRIPS_en.pdf.

———. "United Nations Declaration on the Rights of Indigenous Peoples." 2008. https://www.un.org/development/desa/indigenouspeoples/declaration-on-the-rights-of-indigenous-peoples.html.

———. United Nations Declaration on the Rights of Indigenous Peoples, ga Res 61/295, UNGAOR, 61st Sess, UN Doc a/res/61/295, 2007; United Nations, Economic and Social Council, Commission on Human Rights, Promotion and Protection of Human Rights, Impunity: Report of the Independent Expert to Update the Set of Principles to Combat Impunity, Diane Orentlicher, Addendum: Updated Set of Principles for the Protection and Promotion of Human Rights through Action to Combat Impunity, 61st Sess., Item 17 of the Provisional Agenda, Doc. e/cn.4/2005/102/, February 8, 2005, https://documents-dds-ny.un.org/doc/undoc/gen/g05/109/00/pdf/g0510900.pdf?OpenElement (UNJOP).

University of Waikato. "Mahi Māreikura." https://www.waikato.ac.nz/library/about/student-centre/taonga/mahi-mareikura.

———. "Pei Te Hurinui Jones Papers." O Neherā, Hamilton, New Zealand. https://onehera.waikato.ac.nz/nodes/view/5217.

U.S. Department of State. "Announcement of U.S. Support for the United Nations Declaration on the Rights of Indigenous People." January 12, 2011. https://2009-2017.state.gov/s/srgia/154553.htm.

Waitangi Tribunal. "About the Waitangi Tribunal." *Waitangi Tribunal.* June 16, 2017. https://waitangitribunal.govt.nz/about-waitangi-tribunal/past-present-future-of-waitangi-tribunal.

Wareham, Evelyn. "'Our Own Identity, Our Own Taonga, Our Own Self Coming Back': Indigenous Voices in New Zealand Record-Keeping." *Archivaria* 52 (2001): 26–46.

Whaanga, Hēmi, and Rangiiria Hedley. "The Display and Conservation of Taonga Maori-Establishing Culturally Appropriate Display and Conservation Facilities: Mahi Mareikura-a Work in Progress." *He Puna Korero: Journal of Māori and Pacific Development* 7, no. 2 (2006): 3–39.

Whaanga, Hēmi, David Bainbridge, Michela Anderson, Korii Scrivener, Papitha Cader, Tom Roa, and Te Taka Keegan. "He Matapihi Mā Mua, Mō Muri: The Ethics, Processes, and Procedures Associated with the Digitization of Indigenous Knowledge—The Pei Jones Collection." *Cataloging & Classification Quarterly* 53, no. 5–6 (2015): 520–47.

Williams, Dana A., and Marissa K. Lopez. "More Than a Fever: Toward a Theory of the Ethnic Archive." *PMLA/Publications of the Modern Language Association of America* 127, no. 2 (2012): 357–59.

Wilson, Ian E. "'A Noble Dream': The Origins of the Public Archives of Canada." *Archivaria* 15 (1982): 16–35.

Witchey, Holly. "Tribal Archives, Libraries and Museums: ATALM, a Practical Model for Local Collaboration." In *Economic Considerations for Libraries, Archives and Museums*, edited by Lorraine A. Stuart, Thomas F. R. Clareson, and Joyce Ray, 77–91. New York: Routledge, 2022.

Wolfe, Patrick. "Settler Colonialism and the Elimination of the Native." *Journal of Genocide Research* 8 (2006): 387–409.

Wurrppujinta Anyul Mappu. "A Gathering Place." Last modified 2023. https://wumpurrarni-kari.libraries.wsu.edu/.

Yakel, Elizabeth. "Archival Representation." *Archival Science* 3, no. 1 (2003): 1–25.

Zhang, Jane. "Original Order in Digital Archives." *Archivaria* 74 (2012): 167–93.

About the Authors

KRISTA MCCRACKEN is an award-winning public historian and archivist. They work as a Researcher/Curator at Algoma University's Arthur A. Wishart Library and Shingwauk Residential Schools Centre in Baawating (Sault Ste. Marie, Ontario) on the traditional territory of the Anishinaabe and Métis people. Krista's work focuses on community archives, residential schools, access, and outreach.

Krista is an editor of the popular Canadian history website Activehistory.ca. In 2020, they won the best article in Indigenous History prize awarded by the Canadian Historical Association's Indigenous History Group for their article "Challenging Colonial Spaces: Reconciliation and Decolonizing Work in Canada's Archives."

Krista is currently pursuing their PhD in Library and Information Management via Manchester Metropolitan University and San Jose State University. When not working, they can be found drinking tea, watching *Doctor Who*, and editing Wikipedia. Krista is also an avid embroiderer.

SKYLEE-STORM HOGAN-STACEY is a public historian, researcher, and analyst currently living and working on the unceded territory of the Algonquin Anishinaabek in Ottawa, Ontario. A descendant of the Mohawk Nation of Kahnawà:ke, Skylee-Storm has explored community archival practices, Indigenous archival access, residential school history, Indigenous-Crown legal history, and oral history.

Skylee-Storm began their work with the Shingwauk Residential Schools Centre in 2015 and worked with them until 2018. They have remained a collaborator with the centre on projects related to community archives and site history. Skylee-Storm completed a rewrite of the provincial site history and Ontario Provincial Heritage Program plaque for Shingwauk Hall in 2022.

Skylee-Storm is currently on an interchange with the office of the Independent Special Interlocutor for Missing Children and Unmarked Graves and Burial Sites associated with Indian residential schools and works with their legal and research department as a policy analyst focused on archives, access, and data sovereignty. When they aren't writing, working, or traveling, Skylee-Storm enjoys spending time with their cat, reading mysteries, beading, and embroidery.

Index

A
Aanischaaukamikw Cree Cultural Institute (ACCI), 50–51
Aboriginal and Torres Strait Islander Data Archive (ATSIDA), 51–53
Aboriginal and Torres Strait Islander Library, Information and Resource Network (ATSILIRN), 21
Aboriginal and Torres Strait Islander Protocols for Libraries, Archives and Information Services. *See* ATSILIRN Protocols.
access
  accommodations for, 66
  barriers to, 4, 7, 63
  Indigenous traditional knowledge protocols and, 15
  push for open, 7
Alexander Turnbull Library, 39, 54, 55
Alfred, Gerald Taiaiake, 14
American Library Association, 16, 17
American Philosophical Society (APS), 17
American Philosophical Society (APS) Library, 48
Anderson, Jane, 13
Archives New Zealand, 24, 38–39
Association des archivistes du Québec, 19
Association of Canadian Archivists (ACA), 19, 20
Association of College and Research Libraries (ACRL), 17
Association of Tribal Archives, Libraries, and Museums (ATALM), 62
"Atkinson Letters," 39
ATSILIRN Protocols, 21–23, 25
Australia
  colonial archives in, 6–7
  colonial roots of, xvi
  protocols in, 21–23
  provenance in, 37–38
  selection of for study, xv–xvi
  UNDRIP and, 14, 22
Australian Library and Information Association, 21
Australian National University, 51
Australian Wumpurrarni-kari Archive, 37–38

B
Bak, Greg, 14
Bastian, Jeannette Allis, 32, 41
Battley, Belinda, 47
Blackburn, Fiona, 22, 25
Bosum, Annie, 51
Bringing Them Home name index, 7
Bureau of Indian Affairs, 34

C
Callison, Camille, 62
Canada
  child welfare systems in, 11n26
  colonial archives in, 4–6

Canada *(cont'd)*
  colonial roots of, xvi
  protocols in, 18–21
  provenance in, 35–37
  residential/boarding schools in, xvi, 35–37, 49–50
  selection of for study, xv–xvi
  UNDRIP and, 14
Canadian Association of Archivists, 18–19
Canadian Council of Archives (CCA), 19
Carlisle Indian Industrial School, 34–35
Carlisle Indian School Digital Resource Center, 34–35
Caswell, Michelle, 3
Center for Native American and Indigenous Research (CNAIR), 48
ceremony, respect for, 65
child welfare systems, 11n26
Children of Shingwauk Alumni Association (CSAA), 36–37, 49
church record systems, 35
Cline Library, Northern Arizona University, 17
codes of conduct, 8
community engagement, importance of, 65
community-based archival description
  in Australia, 51–54
  in Canada, 49–51
  decolonizing description and, 56–57
  introduction to, 45–47
  in New Zealand, 54–55
  in United States, 48
community-based scholarship, x, 48
community-centered models, 34–35
community-focused provenance, 33, 35, 39. *See also* provenance
Cooper, Kooramyee, 53
copyright
  Aboriginal and Torres Strait Islander Protocols for Libraries, Archives and Information Services and, 22
  Karuk Tribe and, 33
  multiple forms of provenance and, 65–66
Council of Provincial and Territorial Archivists, 19
Cree culture, 50–51
Croswell, Debra, 9
cultural stewardship protocols, 13, 14, 65

D
decolonization, use of term, xv
descriptive practices
  in Australia, 51–54
  in Canada, 49–51
  decolonizing description and, 56–57
  introduction to, 45–47
  in New Zealand, 54–55
  in United States, 48
digital approaches to provenance, 40–41
Digital Knowledge Sharing program, 48
digital repatriation, 37–38, 63
digitization, 4
Douglas, Jennifer, 33
Drupal content management system (CMS), 39
Dunne, Ashley, 51

E
education, 1–2
Eeyou Istchee community, 50–51

F
faculty representation, 1–2
Faulkhead, Shannon, 6
First Archivist Circle, 15
Fraser, Crystal, 5, 62
French Revolution, 3
futurism, Indigenous, 63

G
Garwood-Houng, Alana, 22, 25
General Assembly Library, 54
Ghaddar, J. J., 3, 5
Gilliland, Anne J., 45–46, 52
graves, from residential schools, xvi. *See also* residential/boarding schools

H
Haberstock, Lauren, 46–47
haka, 39, 40
Harkin, Natalie, 6
Hogan-Stacey, Skylee-Storm, ix, x –xi, xiii–xiv, 36, 49, 63
Huebner, Sharon, 53

I
Iacovino, Livia, 31, 47
Indian Act (Canada), 2, 19
Indian Residential School History and Dialogue Centre (IRSHDC), 35–36

Indigenous futurism, 63
intellectual property
　copyright and, 65–66
　Māori rights and, 24
　ownership of, 8–9
　UNDRIP and, 14–15, 22
intergenerational practice, 65
Irlbacher-Fox, Stephanie, 17
Iwi Hapū Names List, 55

J
Jones, Pei, 55

K
Karuk Tribe, 33–34
Keller, Christian, 32
Koorie Archiving System, 53–54
Koorie Heritage Archive (KHA), 53–54
Koorie Heritage Trust Inc, 53

L
language preservation, 39–40
Library and Archives Canada, 4–6, 18, 19
López, Marissa K., 61
Lorde, Audre, 4

M
Mahi Māreikura, 55
Māori people, 23–24, 25, 54–55
Māori Subject Headings Project, 54–55
Mataatua Declaration on Cultural and Intellectual Property Rights of Indigenous Peoples, 7–8, 24
Mātauranga Māori, 55
McCracken, Krista, ix, x –xi, xiii, 36, 49
McKemmish, Sue, 6, 45–46
Millar, Laura, 32
Morse, Bradford W., 54
Mukurtu, 38, 39, 41

N
National Archives and Records Administration (NARA; United States), 3–4, 35
National Archives (Canada), 5–6
National Archives of Australia (NAA), 6
National Archives (United States), 34–35
National Centre for Truth and Reconciliation (NCTR), 35–36
National Library Act (New Zealand), 54
National Library of New Zealand, 54–55

National Library Service (New Zealand), 54
Native American Archives Section, 17
Nesmith, Tom, 32
New Zealand
　colonial archives in, 7–9
　colonial roots of, xvi
　Māori rights and, 23–24, 25
　protocols in, 23–24
　provenance in, 38–40
　selection of for study, xv–xvi
　UNDRIP and, 14, 24
New Zealand Association of Social Anthropologists, 8
Ngā Ūpoko Tukutuk, 55
Northern Arizona University's Cline Library, 17

O
original order, principle of, 31, 40
over documentation, 6

P
participatory archives, 45–47, 65
participatory description, x, 45–47
Pei Te Hurinui Jones collection, 55
photo identification project, 49–50
postcustodial models, 33, 38
Powell, Timothy B., 48
protocols
　in Australia, 21–23
　in Canada, 18–21
　introduction to, 13
　in New Zealand, 23–24
　in practice, 25
　UNDRIP and, 13–15
　in United States, 15–17
Protocols for Native American Archival Materials (PNAAM), x, 15–17, 22–23, 25, 57
Protocols for the Treatment of Indigenous Materials (APS), 17
provenance
　in Australia, 37–38
　in Canada, 35–37
　digital approaches to, 40–41
　introduction to, 31–33
　multiple forms of, 65–66
　in New Zealand, 38–40
　in United States, 33–35
Public Records Act (New Zealand), 24, 25
Punzalan, Ricardo L., x–xii

R

rangatiratanga (chieftainship), 23
Reconciliation Framework: Response to the Report of the Truth and Reconciliation Commission Taskforce, 19–21
relationship building, 56, 57, 59n45, 64–65
relationship-based approach, 16, 25
Remember the Children: Photo Identification Project, 49–50
repatriation, 37–38, 52, 63
reply, right of, 65
Report of the Royal Commission on Aboriginal Peoples (RCAP), 18
reserve systems, 2
residential/boarding schools
   archival organization and, 35–37
   in Canada, xvi, 35–37, 49–50
   graves attributed to, xvi
   participatory description and, 49–50
   in United States, xvi, 4
respect des fonds, 31
Royal Commission into Aboriginal Deaths in Custody, 6
Russell, Lynette, 6

S

self-determination, right of, 64
settler colonialism, x, xiv–xv, 2
sharing-circle consensus models, 37
Shingwauk Indian Residential School, 36–37
Shingwauk Residential Schools Centre (SRSC), xiii–xiv, 36–37, 49–50
Simpson, Leanne Betasamosake, 63
Sípnuuk Digital Library, Archives, and Museum, 33–34
societal provenance, 32, 41
Society of American Archivists (SAA), 16, 17, 25
songs, 39–40
Steering Committee on Canada's Archives (SCCA), 19
Subject Headings Project, 54–55

T

Tāłtān Nation, 62
Tāmata Toiere digital repository, 39–40
Taranaki people, 38–39
Te Awekotuku, Ngahuia, 8
Te Ipukarea—The National Māori Language Institute, 39–40
Te Puna Mātauranga o Aotearoa, 54–55
Te Reo o Taranaki, 38–39
Thorpe, Kirsten, 22
Todd, Zoe, 5, 62
transformation, areas for, 64–65
Treaty of Waitangi, 7, 23–24, 54
Trouillot, Michel-Rolph, 2, 9
Trust and Technology Project, 53
Truth and Reconciliation Commission of Canada (TRC), 18–20
Tuck, Eve, xv

U

United Nations Declaration on the Rights of Indigenous Peoples (UNDRIP), ix, xvi, 8, 13–15, 18–19, 22, 24, 33, 64
United Nations Joinet-Orentlicher Principles (UNJOP), 18–19
United States
   child welfare systems in, 11n26
   colonial archives in, 3–4
   colonial roots of, xvi
   protocols in, 15–17
   provenance in, 33–35
   residential/boarding schools in, xvi, 4
   selection of for study, xv–xvi
   UNDRIP and, 14
University of Michigan, x
University of Melbourne, 51
University of Queensland, 51
University of Waikato, 55
University of Western Australia, 51

W

waiata, 39–40
Waitangi Treaty, 7, 23–24, 54
Waitangi Tribunal, 7, 23
Wareham, Evelyn, 7, 62
white supremacy, 3, 4, 32, 61
Williams, Dana A., 61

Y

Yakel, Elizabeth, 41
Yang, K. Wayne, xv
Younging, Greg, 13

Z

Zhang, Jane, 40

www.ingramcontent.com/pod-product-compliance
Lightning Source LLC
Chambersburg PA
CBHW061420300426
44114CB00015B/2000